THE TIBBLESTONE HUNDRED

*Journey Through An
English Village*

THE
TIBBLESTONE
HUNDRED

*Journey Through An
English Village*

FRED ARCHER

SUTTON PUBLISHING

First published in the United Kingdom in 1996
Sutton Publishing Limited
Phoenix Mill · Far Thrupp · Stroud · Gloucestershire

British Library Cataloguing in Publication Data

A catalogue record of this book is available from the British Library.

ISBN 0-7509-1256-1

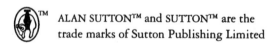

ALAN SUTTON™ and SUTTON™ are the trade marks of Sutton Publishing Limited

Typeset in 12/15 Garamond.
Typesetting and origination by
Sutton Publishing Limited.
Printed in Great Britain by
Hartnolls, Bodmin, Cornwall.

CONTENTS

PREFACE

This books tells the story of the evolution of that small part of
Britain known as the Tibblestone Hundred. It covers a great
number of years, from the time when the hill land was nothing but
unproductive scrub, yet still a refuge for its people from the marches
of the Vale, the flooded Carrants Brook, the River Isbourne. Step by
step after Inclosure a different countryside and people emerge until
we reach the present-day villages and their productive farming
methods.

My wife Elsie, who has worked hard with the script, has never
lived in Tibblestone, yet she has skilfully put the events in order,
having gained, over the last ten years, a feel for this part of the
countryside. Her grandfather farmed the black soil of Lancashire
near Mawdesley where her mother worked as a Land Girl in the
First World War, and where spring cabbages and leeks grow as they
do in the Vale of Evesham. Quite a connection. I'm very grateful to
Elsie for helping to make this book a living social history, the story
of real people.

Fred Archer
1996

INTRODUCTION

Some may rightly question why. Why should we bother about our ancestral land, those of us for whom Bredon Hill and the Hundred of Tibblestone is home? Does it matter who occupied this small corner situated on the Worcestershire/Gloucestershire border so long ago? Does it matter about their lives and the stories they could tell? I believe that it does matter, because these folk and their experiences form the basis of our culture today.

As all over this small island, the folk of Bredon Hill are a mixture of races. Meeting families who have lived under the shadow of the Hill for centuries I detect certain traits in their faces and physique. Some have a Roman appearance, some are blonde and Saxon, but the ones who intrigue me most are the short, dark, swarthy type, those whose origins may lie over the border in Wales, and who have a similar make-up to the ancient Silures tribe. Indeed, the folk of Bredon and the Tibblestone are a mixed race, it's true, bordering on Wales, close to the Midlands, yet we tend to think of ourselves as belonging to the South-West.

During the Civil War, the Tibblestone, midway between Gloucester and Worcester, stood between King Charles, supported by Worcester, and the Commonwealth, supported by Gloucester. A fine line marked the two armies. Just over the border from Tibblestone, at Elmley Castle, the villagers supported the king and at nearby Kersoe a farmer named Moore is said to have drawn a wagon load of hay across the road to hinder the army of the Commonwealth en route to the Battle of Worcester.

Villages in the Tibblestone Hundred were actually all in the county of Gloucestershire. The county boundaries were so crooked before they were straightened in 1931 that driving along the road one was never sure which county one was in after all. Even today some counties treat their roads so much better than their neighbours.

Despite the confusion over boundaries, a certain parochialism did exist between neighbouring villages in Gloucestershire and Worcestershire when I was a boy. We folk in Ashton under Hill didn't mix much with Sedgeberrow, a Worcestershire village, apart from the necessary trading arrangements. Sedgeberrow people didn't like us very much. Ashton under Hill men were farmers and Sedgeberrow, on better land, grew fruit and vegetables for market.

At Ashton under Hill the older villagers clung to their association with Gloucestershire and their post town of Tewkesbury. One villager, a descendant of the Baldwyn family who had lived in the village for six hundred years, told me about the time when the boundary was changed, and we were transferred to Worcestershire: 'That's a bad move; now we are a part of the Midlands and will be influenced by Birmingham.' This same man once went on a mystery tour by coach. As the coach passed through Evesham he closed his eyes. Strong feelings from this member of that well-known family. We are, as you may gather, an independent race in the villages under the Hill.

On my visits to Sedgeberrow on Saturday mornings in the 1920s, to the blacksmith's with two cart horses tied nose to tail in tandem, it felt as if I was travelling to a foreign land. Tom, the blacksmith who owned the smithy, was suspicious of our village folk in general, and the bartering over the quarterly bill for shoeing the cart horses was a source of entertainment for us boys. Tom was a great friend of Dad, despite the feelings between the villages. They would sit by the fireside, Dad aiming for as much discount as possible on the amount of the bill and Tom steadfastly holding his ground. A compromise was always agreed on. I also took oats and dray loads of corn to be ground for the cattle at Sedgeberrow Watermill. This mill was one of many on the River Isbourne, and the ancient mechanism intrigued me.

Elmley Castle in Worcestershire with the hamlet of Kersoe between there and Ashton under Hill – we didn't mix with them!

Did it go back to the time of Cromwell and King Charles, when Worcestershire was for the king, and we Gloucesters were for Cromwell? Since the time that Moore's wagon delayed Cromwell's army, men of Elmley walk proudly about the parish with long nut walking sticks. What have we, the Cromwellians, got to counter such tales? Didn't Oliver Cromwell tie his horse up at Camp House in the little hamlet of Paris on Bredon Hill above Ashton? The iron ring was still there, fixed into the half timbers, when I was a boy. In latter years when the railway from Birmingham to Ashchurch, known as the Loop Line, was built, Beckford, Ashton under Hill and Hinton on the Green all had their stations; maybe Sedgeberrow and Elmley Castle felt left out in the cold.

I suppose most folk are conversant with the term to apply for The Chiltern Hundreds. It is when a Member of Parliament resigns their office. England was divided up into Hundreds consisting of a group of villages and land as early as AD 939 during the reign of King Edmund. A Hundred was a unit of local government, somewhere between the village and the shire in size and importance. Tibblestone Hundred consisted of Beckford, Ashton under Hill, Grafton, Hinton on the Green, Didcot, a part of Dumbleton, Teddington and Bengrove, 6,773 acres in all.

Vestry meetings held at Parish churches preceded Parish Councils, and Hundred Courts held monthly were a mixture between District Council Meetings and Petty Sessions. These Hundred Courts, held to settle private disputes, took place in the open air; the judged had to be tenants of the Hundred. The designated venue was either at the Hundred Stone or the Hundred Tree.

In the Tibblestone Hundred, the Hundred Stone was known as The Tibblestone. It stands today near the junction of five roads at a spot known as Teddington Hands. A stone finger-post nearby points to Cheltenham, Evesham, Stow-on-the-Wold, Tewkesbury and Overbury. It was moved slightly in 1949 to make way for a roundabout.

These large irregular marking stones have always been the subject of folklore. In the pre-Christian era superstition was a part of everyday life. The story goes of a giant living on Bredon Hill going up above Tibblestone to fetch a large stone to destroy his enemy's house. Coming down the hill carrying the stone, his foot slipped and his heel made a big furrow on the hillside, which it is said can be seen today. He had to drop the stone at Teddington crossroads. The holes in the stone are the marks where the giant's fingers had held it. It has always seemed to me that the area known as Tibblestone Hundred, which included a part of Bredon Hill, has had a mystic feel about it from the time of the Druids. This strangeness continued down through the ages and early in the twentieth century superstition among the folk of the Hundred was rife.

In the Bible we read 'Remove not the ancient landmarks which your fathers have set up'. If a stone is moved it's said to be the work of Jack o' Lantern, the Will-o'-the-Wisp, who was in league with the Devil. It must have been quite scary for our ancestors, this Will-o'-the-Wisp, an eerie light on the flat lands, swamps, by the river and brook. Modern science explains this phenomenon as being connected with phosphorous. Our ancestors never knew what the fiery ghost was; some called it 'Kit with the Candlestick'. It was like a wisp or bunch of straw glowing, a straw torch on marshy ground, a phosphorous-like light. The technical term is *ignis fatuus*, meaning foolish fire, because of its strange, erratic movement. Perhaps it was caused by phosphorous weeds on swampy ground. Whatever, it was a terror to travellers at night.

George, our under-carter, was always afraid of dark mornings when he fetched his team from the Carrants Brook meadows and he would pay his school-boy brother a penny to accompany him, for once George had seen Jack o' Lantern. The superstition of our ancestors, when the unexplained was a part of country life, certainly made it less dull.

The Bredon Hill villages today, Beckford and Ashton under Hill in particular, are very different from the usual Cotswold village with its Cotswold-stone buildings. Overbury is built in the main in Cotswold-type stone, from the quarries on Bredon maybe, but most likely from Stanway across the Vale. Beckford and Ashton under

Hill mainly have timber-built houses. The great elms of the clay land under the Hill made timber building a feature in the Middle Ages. Why use stone when the timber was on the spot?

Stone from the quarries on the Hill was used for the picturesque walls around the hill fields and for making the roads around the Hill. The circular route between the Avon river and the foot hills is about 19 miles long, running through Beckford, Grafton, Ashton under Hill, Kersoe, Elmley Castle, The Combertons, Eckington, Bredons Norton, Westmancote, Kemerton, Overbury and Conderton. The soil is particularly rich around the Eckington area, possibly due to the flooding of the River Avon. It is here that early market garden crops have been grown to supply the needs of Birmingham. Further afield, where the Severn runs through Longdon Marsh, there was a great wildlife sanctuary before it was drained. All types of waterfowl inhabited this marsh land.

What a change on Bredon Hill itself! The Hill in my lifetime grew very little, and years before was a land of trees, scrub, hawthorn and gorse, infested with rabbits. No need to cut a road around the oats on Bredon for the binder at harvest, the rabbits grazed the headland and more. Now the rabbits are few compared with pre-myxomatosis days and with modern farming methods barley grows to perfection. A few years ago I walked around Great Hill Barn, one of my favourite haunts of youth, and had difficulty in making my way along the headland of a field of oil seed rape. The crop was fantastic and tree-like – this is a revolution, I thought, compared with the scant crops of yesterday. As the saying goes 'There's gold in them there Hills'.

Before the time of the Inclosures of 1773 families had grazing rights on the Hill to keep animals, a cow maybe, pigs in the woods, and geese on the common land. The men worked on the farms and estates but had days off to cultivate their own strips of arable land. There was some independence. This all changed when the land was enclosed. After that, farmers employed the men as labourers.

During the early Victorian period men were treated like slaves, paid only 9 or 10s a week. They reaped, they mowed, they threshed with the flail, life was grim. Farmers were doing quite well until the wet summer of 1879, when the majority of their sheep died with liver fluke. At that time the Game Laws were so strict that a labourer dared not kill even a rabbit in his own garden.

At the turn of the century the Church that owned many acres of Glebe land began to rent out smallholdings to the villagers of Ashton under Hill, Hinton on the Green and Beckford, three villages in the Tibblestone Hundred. Holdings of 5 or 6 acres were eagerly snapped up by the young men of the villages. Independence was regained by some, at least. These men grew their crops of fruit and vegetables for market. Some grew an acre of wheat and had it ground into flour for breadmaking at the mills on the River Isbourne. A clan of Little Master Men evolved thanks to the Church. The Ashton smallholders had land at Ayles Acre and Hill Withy. It was hand work and hard work, but these pioneers altered the life in the villages for fifty years or more. When we talk of independence, the Little Master Men it is true had more. They had a certain selfishness, a stubborn instinct of possession. They had either a conscious or sub-conscious dread that they would experience what their ancestors had done in 1773 and lose their land. Six acres of land and unbeholden to any master was worth fighting for. The farmers of the Hundred had mixed feelings about the smallholders. Some did lend a couple of horses for them to plough an acre or so; others thought the men of the holdings were a threat.

As tenant smallholders nearly every man kept a dog and carried a gun. As they laboured in winter and summer their dogs lay on their master's coat on the headland beside the gun. Some did a little poaching but in the main their fur and feather was rabbits and pigeons for the pot. Organized poaching from gangs in nearby towns was different. They poached to sell. The smallholders worked silently on the Hill, with the long net quietly taking rabbits. Some farmers welcomed these men who kept down the crop-eating pests.

Superstition and suspicion went side-by-side in the homes and on the holdings of these pioneers. Crops were planted on Saints Days, potatoes on Good Friday, whether it was early or late. Some planted when the moon was waxing, others when the moon was waning. The men were dubious about artificial fertilizers but were great believers in household soot on the heavy land. The intention of the market gardeners was to get their crops to market early, a week before their neighbours. They were competitive alright. By selection, one man grew early wallflowers, but was careful to keep his own seed. A conversation might go like this: Bert would say to Alf, 'Could you spare a little wallflower seed?' Alf's reply would be, 'I be just off to bed, thee bist too late.' It meant 'No'. Alf's seed was for himself.

The men of the three villages, keen to better one another, had their tricks in ripening their plums. They picked them under-ripe and 'stived' them, covering the baskets with paper and keeping them in their warm kitchens. Their fruit then was ready for market a week early. One of the bad facets of marketing in those days was the system of 'topping' their fruit for market. All the best strawberries were placed on top of the punnets or baskets, the inferior ones hidden underneath.

Where to send their produce from the local railway station was a problem. Growers were secretive about good markets in the north of England. Some growers made notes of the labels on their neighbours' produce and arranged to send supplies to those merchants in the hope of beating them to it.

One can understand the attitude of these men, trying to keep their independence meant looking after their own interests, but the selfishness and suspicion went by the board when neighbours were ill and unable to work. It is recorded that a group of smallholders dug a neighbour's holding one Sunday when the man was ill enabling him to plant his crops in the spring.

Life was like that in the Tibblestone Hundred. It was a place full of characters, all individuals, some quite eccentric, as shall be seen. All the residents of the Hundred though shared the common love of life on the land of yesterday.

CHAPTER ONE

THE ROADS IN
THE TIBBLESTONE

The Lower Deviation Saltway was just one of the original Roman
trackways along which pannier-loaded horses took that vital
commodity, salt, from Droitwich to the south coast of England.
Here it was shipped over to Gaul. To plot its route we start at
Pershore, then travel through Little Comberton, Bricklehampton,
Elmley Castle and through Netherton, past the Saltway Barn to
Hinton Roughs, which is where the Saltway entered Tibblestone.
The route descended Furze Hill Bank to Ashton under Hill, to a
section known as Rycknield Street. The track through Ashton then
took a line down Gipsies Lane, past Didcot Ham, the part of the
Parish allied to Didcot, where it left Tibblestone, going on to
Sudeley Castle en route for Northleach and eventually reaching the
coast at Seaton in Devon.

We do tend to think of the Romans making straight roads, and it
is true that the military roads were often virtually straight. The
Roman Road crossing the Cotswolds at Birdlip drops down to the
Vale in a more or less straight line. But the Saltway used by the
packhorses took the lie of the land into account, skirting the
steepest hills, following the track that the animals would take
instinctively.

Bredon Hill appears to have been a staging post where the horses
stayed on their way south. A great amphitheatre above Ashton
Wood was known as the Horse Camps, and the animals stayed here
overnight, guarded from the wild beasts that roamed the
countryside during that period. Below, on a level plain, there is a
piece of land known as the Pavement, a Biblical term. And the

names of some of the fields have also remained: Nosterns Well, Hell Hole, Upper Saltway Piece, and Saltway Barn Piece (this field is on the route from Netherton to Hinton Roughs).

Overlooking the Saltway a long slope on Bredon, known as Starn Hill, reaches from the Pound Hill high on Bredon down to Ashton Wood. Between Starn Hill and the Saltway there are pieces of land known as Throughters and Moll Hays.

There is speculation about the destination of these pannier-loaded animals when they reached the Fosse Way near Northleach. Some say the route took a course to Lechlade, where the salt was loaded on boats on the Thames for London.

Later, Beckford succumbed to the Saxon Invasion. The Saxons were converted to Christianity and soon there was a mission station or a monastery at Beckford. The Saxon Chronicle for Worcestershire refers to Beckford as Beccanford in AD 803. But it was in the eighteenth century that road development really took place, and this led in turn to the establishment of the Evesham Road Club.

In 1788 the roads in the Bredon Hill area, some in the Hundred of Tibblestone, were particularly bad. Farmers using narrow-wheeled wagons did a lot of damage to the roads. These farm wagons, with wheels less than six inches wide, were banned from the roads by the Club, with a fine of £5 if this rule was broken. The first rule of the Road Club was that everyone joining the society must accede to an agreement of the inhabitants of Beckford, Overbury, Kemerton and Bredon entered on 18 September 1788, in the following terms:

We the undersigned inhabitants of Beckford, Overbury, Kemerton and Bredon feeling very sensibly the inconvenience arising from the bad state of the roads in our neighbourhood and wishing to act cordially and unitedly in the best manner for the improvement of the said roads to declare that it is our intention by advice and example to put the law relating thereto in strict execution and for this purpose we will be ready and willing to serve (at least on our term) as Surveyors of the roads in our respective parishes and we strongly recommend to the parishioners to appoint such persons as shall be most likely to execute the duties of that office with regularity impartiality and diligence.

Signed: William Wakeman, John Darke, James Martin, R. Speederman, John Parsons, Henry White, J. Biddle, Roger Parry, William Hicks, William Freeman, Thomas Gibbs, Charles Tidmarsh, John Bricknell, John Allcock, Isaac Nind.

The Vale of Evesham Road Club mainly consisted of members who were residents in the neighbourhood of Bredon Hill. The members met on the first Thursday of the month at half past two at inns in the area, the Crown at Evesham, the Angel at Pershore, the White Hart at Winchcombe. The rules of the Club were printed on a large paper and framed, fixed and displayed in the hall or the most frequented rooms in the houses of the members, as well as on the church doors and in the market-places. Advice was available for the Surveyors about road construction and maintenance. Only weathered stone was to be used, weathered for at least twelve months. Drainage was important for surface water to run to the roadside ditches.

Before the Road Club was formed, little was done to improve the roads in the Bredon Hill area. Many may assume that the A495 Evesham to Cheltenham road had always been a fairly straight run between the Cotswolds and Bredon. That is not so. The road was virtually non-existent until 1789. In May's *History of Evesham* the following information is recorded:

In 1789 in the reign of George III by an Act directing the division of Evesham roads into certain districts the Trustees were discharged from the management of the road to Hinton on the Green leading towards Tewkesbury as mentioned in the First Act. This was as you can gather three years before the Evesham Road Club was formed. The same year an Act was passed amending the Tewkesbury Road from Hampton Turnpike towards Teddington Cross beyond Beckford Inn and then joining the Stow to Tewkesbury Road.

This road from Hampton was a major breakthrough in communications because previous to the construction of this new road, the only way to get to Tewkesbury from Hinton on the Green was via the old road over Bredon Hill, which ran on to Pigeon Lane, Conderton, and then went on to Kemerton and Tewkesbury. Despite its steep incline, this old road over Bredon did have the advantage of being a hill road, running high above the flood valley of the rivers Carrant and Isbourne. The land from Hinton to Teddington was low-lying ground and subject to flooding from these rivers.

In the late eighteenth century the road from Ashton under Hill Turnpike to Sedgeberrow was known as Umberlands Lane. This is of great interest to me because I worked a lot of my life on a field known as Umberlands Length, a fairly narrow field going from the Umberland Lane to the boundary of Dumbleton Parish. It was 220 yards long or ten chains, easy to measure because every chain width was an acre of land.

Umberlands Length was adjacent to the Big Thurness or Giant Nose. If ever a field had a descriptive name it was this one, for the field is indeed shaped like a giant nose. It stands alongside the Needlelands, two fields narrow and long like needles lying alongside Carrants Brook.

Further towards Beckford Inn the road from Hinton was called Dewrest Lane. Again my land ran alongside with three meadows, the Long Dewrest, the Middle Dewrest and the Little Dewrest. These meadows, aptly named, were drenched with dew on summer hay-making mornings.

In the late nineteenth century the village roads were maintained by a roadman who used stone off Bredon Hill. Joe Barnet dug the limestone off Holcombe Knap and was paid by the ton. The duties of the roadmen varied, and some took on extra work too. Samuel Jones was the roadman who maintained the roads from Ashton under Hill through Grafton to Beckford. A strong Chapel man with an enormous nose, the village lads, on passing him, used to walk by on the grass verge, saying, 'Think there's room to get by him?'.

Samuel's job was to cut the roadside verges with his scythe and shovel up the horse manure left by the teams of work horses. This was good for the gardens – petrol engines today don't leave this bonus.

Stodge Warren did some stone breaking, wearing gauze goggles to protect his eyes, and leaving heaps of stones at the roadside. Sometimes he was spotted sitting on them, resting from his labours.

The village roads at the turn of the century were full of wheel ruts made by the farm carts and wagons. Dad rode a cushion-tyred bicycle down those wheel ruts. Grandfather had a donkey and cart which my father used to take produce from the market garden to Evesham market. In those days the growers provided their own hampers which meant that Dad took all day doing the 6 miles each way to town, for he had the empties to collect after the market sale. Coming home on those dark evenings with the donkey was quite a thing as at every little noise in the hedge the donkey stopped, his long ears pointing to the rustle of the leaves, a bird, a field mouse. The carrot on the stick to entice Neddy was a reality!

The breakthrough came when Dad bought a Bradbury motor bike at an auction. It was a heavy machine with a primitive ignition. There was no magneto but a battery which often went dead, leaving him stranded miles from home. He used to have to put the bike on the train. Dad was a pioneer motor cyclist, riding as early as 1910, with his cap back to front and sporting goggles, and there are many stories about his adventures with his bike. I remember it resting by the hay loader in the barn with its bulbous horn, blown quite often by the little boy who writes this story. Although not common, I remember another motor bike too. Percy Wigley, a retired engineer from Birmingham, had a Douglas motor bike which he powered with paraffin. Talk about pollution! Percy made a smoke screen right up the village street.

But transport then was mainly provided by the horse, pulling traps, Governess Cars, drays, carrier carts. The roads of Tibblestone were still the scene of horse power, creaky wagons, the jingle of harness, bakers' carts, butchers' wagons, the oil man's travelling shop, which sold everything from mousetraps to chamber pots!

Mr Bailey, Dad's partner, had a fast, iron-grey, cob. It took several men to catch this animal whenever Mr Bailey wanted to go to town. But what a turn-out he made, with the polished black, brass-mounted harness. Our cob, named Polly, was a liver chestnut, a quiet mare, who earned little boys a penny to mind in Evesham Market-place on shopping days.

Mr Nicklin, an iron master from the Black Country, had a Sunbeam car, 1913 vintage, and a chauffeur in green livery, but he often took the train first class to Birmingham, smoking a Churchill-sized cigar. He was a friend of my father's, both true blue Tories.

Doctor Roberson with his pony and trap was a feature in the village, but not before lunch time. He visited folk at night, saw them at their worst. Lavender, his cob, was always ready, patiently waiting for him. Henry Fly by Night would harness him in the morning and tie him to the rails outside the Doctor's house, where he would be ready for the night-time dashes. Then the Doctor bought a car, a Britain with wooden spokes, a sickly yellow colour. His son Buckram drove, but the Doctor still often went by Lavender and the trap.

Soon Mr Bailey and Dad followed suit; Mr Bailey sold his cob, Dad sold Polly, and both invested in motor cars. The peace of the village was marred by the noise of engines, the air polluted by petrol fumes.

It was March 1923 when Ernest Roberts went to London by train with my father to collect a 1914 Sunbeam, 16 horsepower car. Ernest drove it part way the 100 miles home then Dad took over. He had only ever driven a Fordson tractor before. He told me, 'We touched thirty miles an hour along the Cheltenham road' as the grey and black tourer was driven back to the farm yard. Here was something from the London Car Mart. The stable wall was knocked down to make what Dad called the Motor House. He bought the first pair of wellingtons I'd ever seen, and a hose pipe to clean the car. Its brass radiator, side screens, running-boards, and spare petrol can were quality-made in Wolverhampton, but the sound of the Klaxon horn was enough to scare anyone.

This Sunbeam car was a far cry from the cars of today. The black painted mudguards were polished with Cherry Blossom boot polish and, of course, the wooden spokes in the wheels could get dry and shrink. In summer time the hose pipe was handy for spraying water on the spokes to tighten them.

Soon after the car's arrival, it was used to take loads of sprouts, peas and strawberries along the road past the Tibblestone and on to Cheltenham Market. The produce was piled into the back of the car, which had its back seat removed. That was not all. Saturdays to Gloucester Market, me on the front seat and a load of calves in the back, was a weekly trip with the Sunbeam. The calves seemed happy in the back of the car, in fact one I was holding persisted in licking Dad's ear as we drove home. Sometimes the calves were put into Gobsell Brown corn sacks. They travelled well that way and the car stayed reasonably clean. Other days I held the calves on halters and remember one particular Saturday holding four calves that way. These calves were about a week old, brought straight from their mother cows for rearing on our nurse cows.

The roads through Tibblestone were still quiet compared with today. Some drays and spring carts took produce to the Evesham and Pershore markets, but the road through Kersoe to Elmley Castle still had grass growing up the middle in the days when we would take a Sunday afternoon walk out of the village.

During the rail strike of 1926, by then having learnt to ride a bike, I would cycle the 6 miles to school on an 18 inch frame bike. I really took to the road when I bought a Hercules model, complete with chromium-plated handlebars, for £3 19s 6d in 1931. This bike took me to football and cricket matches in Tibblestone and beyond, and riding back home on those frosty winter nights, I remember thinking that I had finally arrived. The King of the Road oil lamp gave more smoke than light but who cared, I was legitimate.

The roads were improving and Tarmac came to Tibblestone. Hard Clee Hill stone replaced the limestone off the hill. Buses ran on these improved roads now; some took the natives of Tibblestone just over the border of that Hundred to Toddington, where Hugh Andrews had planted the largest acreage of fruit trees ever attempted in England. The fruit-pickers told me stories of Lord Sudeley, an eccentric gentleman who built a spiral staircase in that mansion, from the library to his bedroom at the top of the house. Why, when a grand staircase served the other bedrooms? Because he didn't want anyone to know what time he went to bed!

As carts and wagons had given way to cars and buses, so these vehicles were to give way to the train, and the middle part of the century certainly was the Age of the Train, the railway age. And sure enough, the railway came to the Tibblestone Hundred, just as it reached all across the country. In a later chapter I describe some of the effects it had on the area, as well as some of the characters involved with it.

But it is ironic how things often turn full circle. Now, with the network of motorways spreading all the time, we find ourselves coming back to the roads – roads to rail to roads. And it's a pity really that travelling by rail is no longer as popular as it once was.

CHAPTER TWO

FIELD NAMES

THE THURNESS AND THE GIANT NOSE

Field names have been essential as well as picturesque and descriptive. When the workers on the land had little education it was pointless for their employer to tell them to plough Ordnance Reference 103. The Big Thurness, they knew from boyhood where that field was. It was that heavy clay field of 21 acres, 2 roods and 19 perches on the boundary of the Tibblestone Hundred. The name Thurness, or Thorness, describes the field so nicely, 'Thor' being a giant and 'ness' a nose shape. Places like Wrabness and Walton on the Naze are all nose-shaped.

Ralph and I ploughed the Big Thurness in the winter of 1931. The 21 acres took us a month, with four horses in line. The clay came up as big as a horse's head, rippling from the furrow like slices of frying bacon. Ralph was at the plough tails and I walked the furrow side, complete with a ploughman's whip, the cracking of which resembled the explosion of a .22 rifle. Horses and men working together like this was a common sight on the Gloucestershire land in the early twentieth century. Ralph would always have his clay pipe, puffing the smoke made by Red Bell Shag tobacco, and me, in my early teens, with the occasional Woodbine.

'Cup Turpin. Cup Captain. Cup Flower.' Boxer, slack-traced as usual, was passenger in the team. I cracked the whip, shouting at this liver chestnut. But Boxer was Ralph's ewe lamb favourite of the team, and my action brought strong words from Ralph, 'Don't thee whip that hoss, he's doing his shot.'

Ralph was a shortish man, spare yet strong. He wore a grey jacket, a trilby hat, cord trousers. He walked the furrow as if he had corns, but on the road he swayed with a nautical roll. Always on the go, not resting on the headland apart from lighting his pipe. Work was his life, and the horses his interest, apart from bell ringing and singing at concerts. When the work went well he sang or whistled. If it went badly he blamed the weather, or his aged team: 'Thee Dad ought to buy me some young horses. These be getting past it.' I heard this often; young horses never came, although in time a 20 horsepower Fordson tractor did.

Ralph at the plough tails earned something over 30*s* a week; my wage was 11*s*. I'm prepared to say we earned every penny. So long ago, the winter and spring were probably very wet, and clay needs frost to lax it into a tilth. The Thurness needed strong cultivation in March. The wind had dried the clay into clods. Larkworthys of Worcester made a cultivator we called a scuffle. It had nine tines, each tine had a long stem coming from an iron frame, and was fitted with a stick-pointed share. It took four horses to pull a Larkworthy Scuffle.

It was Friday morning. Ralph and I were in the stable when Mr Harry Bailey, Dad's partner, came into the yard. Every morning on the extension telephone Dad and Harry planned the day for their men. 'Ralph,' the Gaffer called, 'Take four horses and the Larkworthy Scuffle and scuffle the Thurness with young Fred.'

We hitched Flower and Pleasant, the two mares, double onto the front of the implement, Boxer and Turpin all in traces were put in front of them. The mares were connected with a coupling stick between mullions (bridles). Boxer and Turpin had coupling chains between them. Ralph guided the Filler mares with rope reins and I led Turpin on the near side of the team. The Scuffle rocked and rolled over the clay like a ship on choppy water as the tines broke the furrowed land. On the headland Turpin was headstrong, more than once he stepped on my feet, an animal nearly a ton in weight.

This is farming, I thought, when by knocking-off time my legs felt like the clay they walked on. A clod-hopper rightly named, with hob-nailed boots, heavy but substantial. On Saturday night in town I found South African field boots on sale for 12*s* 6*d*. Buying a pair, I felt that I was really set up. But the next week was a disaster. The boots fell apart in a couple of days. The clods were the cause.

The scuffling finished it was decided to fallow the Thurness and Ralph followed the scuffling with three horses abreast pulling duckfoot drags. He drove his team with reins.

Alongside the Thurness lay a field known as Umberlands Length. The road at the one end was Umberlands Lane. Dad used to say that the real name of that long narrow field was 'Hammer and Length'. It puzzles me still.

CONEY BURROWS

At the foot of Bredon Hill the field known as Coney Burrows was also called the Doctor's Hill. Coney Burrows lies beneath some slip land where the limestone is honeycombed with rabbit holes. This field had the wood on one side and a field known as Gossle bordering the other side, which is now a housing estate called Gorse Hill.

Doctor Roberson, a great shot with his gun, kept the rabbits down on Coney Burrows. On the hill above, deer escaping from Elmley Wood often came down to Coney Burrows, trimming the gorse bushes. On the edge of night, Doctor Roberson's workman, Arthur Soden, said, 'Doctor, there's a deer up on your hill anant the Gossle hedge.'

Without a pause the medical man was creeping up the side of the hedge with his gun. A brown figure stood under the hedge. Nearer and nearer the Doctor moved to what Arthur had said was a deer. Bang went the cartridge from the gun and the marksman expecting the animal to fall discovered that he had shot at a cow crib.

In a village these things are mulled over in the pub. A couple of days after this a man came to the Plough and Harrow buying rags and bones and rabbit skins. One wag, a customer at the inn, said, 'Sorry, we've got no rabbit skins, but over the road the Doctor lives and he has got a very fine deer skin.'

The man went over to the surgery with the message he had heard. What Doctor Roberson said to him or the customers at the Plough and Harrow is not worth repeating.

So the field known as Coney Burrows had memories. Rabbits, no doubt, are still there among the gorse bushes, which are ever in bloom.

PECKED MEADOW

Pecked Meadow is a field of 10 acres, 24 perches. It is common on the Gloucestershire–Worcestershire border to refer to an object or a field as being 'pecked' instead of 'pointed'. Pecked Meadow is, like so many of the old inclosures, an odd shape. It lies between the Old Midland Railway line and the main Cheltenham Road, formerly called Umberlands Lane.

The field used to flood very badly from the Carrants Brook. I fetched cattle from there one winter when it was knee-deep in water. This was the field where Buckram, the Midnight Milkman, took a short cut leaving the gate open for Dick, his nag, to graze the mowing grass. The owner of the field said to him, 'Keep your horse out of my mowing grass.'

The cute milkman replied, 'That horse does not belong to me, it belongs to the old Doctor.'

Now the Doctor had been dead for three years, but Charles, the farmer, having a sense of humour, replied, 'Well Buckram, how do I contact him? Is he playing a harp or shovelling coal?'

Pecked Meadow has now been drained; I see tomatoes and other glasshouse crops for sale. A farm shop stands by a bungalow at the main roadside.

DEWREST

A lot of thought must have gone into some of the field names. Men looked at nature, took time to stand and stare and think. What could be more apt than the names of the three fields called Dewrest. The Long Dewrest, a field of over 11 acres, had a right-angled bend, the two fields alongside were the Middle Dewrest and the Little Dewrest. I farmed these fields for a number of years and was conscious of the dew resting on those low-lying meadows in the early mornings. The land was very wet here; when three German bombs were dropped on the Long Dewrest during the Second World War, the craters soon filled with water.

It was only possible to plant spring-sown crops on this land so potatoes seemed a good idea for the Long Dewrest. The Majestic variety grew reasonably well but there was one snag, the potatoes simply refused to soften in the water when boiled. I sold a load to a neighbour for his pigs and he promised to take another load the following week. But meeting him in the road later he said to me, 'Don't thee bring me any more of those taters. I have boiled them and boiled them and they won't go soft.'

THE STOCKING AND VAN DIEMAN'S LAND

Over in Worcestershire, adjoining Tibblestone, Mr Bagnall had a sort of hobby farm. He employed a cowman, a chauffeur and another chap on his small acreage. Two of his fields next to Tibblestone were called the Stocking and Van Dieman's Land. (Van Dieman's Land was the original name for Tasmania, named after the Dutch admiral who had supervised the expedition during which the country was discovered.)

The Stocking puzzled me a while, for the little field looked nothing like a stocking. The name apparently came from Stockade, a wood. I knew it as a useful little arable field.

Did Van Dieman's Land have connections with transportation to Australasia, which went on in the last century? Well, old systems die hard, and one carter I knew used to say, if the horses' shoulders were sore or pinched, 'We could get transported for this. I'll go to Hanover if we couldn't.'

Hanover, I thought, referred to something way back in history, but it turned out to be George the carter's way of remembering some other George. (He meant those three Georges, the Hanoverian kings.)

CALVES' GORE

Calves' Gore on the road to Beckford is a pasture field near Pinch Loaf Cottages, now called Hill View, where a baker lived. This man gave short weight with his loaves and his house became called Pinch

Loaf. Calves' Gore sounds like the gory end of some poor calf bleeding to death. Of course it's nothing of the kind. This field obviously was suited for grazing by calves and because of its shape it earned the name Calves' Gore, a gore being a term often used by dressmakers for the shape of a skirt, narrower at one point than another.

CINDER MEADOW AND FINCHES PIECE

The names of two fields I knew very well were obscure to me. Why was that big field on the Saltway called Cinder Meadow? So often have I seen whole fields being burnt after harvest, especially after a crop of beans. It was common practice to skim-plough the stubble, called bean brash, and burn it. Our cowman Tom told me that unwelcome insects lived in the hollow stems of the horse bean plants, and also that the ash, the cinders, could be used as a fertilizer. Cinder Meadow, that big field, was away from the rest of the farm, hence it was also known as Set Asunder Meadow.

Along the road at Grafton is a field called the Butts. Doesn't that imply shooting: guns, bows and arrows? It's rather disappointing to learn that the Butts is a field abutting, next to, the village.

So we turn to that little 3½ acres near Carrants Brook called Finches Piece. I have seen the goldfinches on Bredon feeding on the autumn seed heads of the great boar thistle, thistles which were said to be big enough to tie a horse to, thistles quite distinct to the hill country, so prickly that the sheep were deprived of the grazing around their stems, and so invasive that women were employed with stock axes to try to prevent the spreading of this beautiful, purple-headed plant.

Finches Piece is a pretty name, but to me it doesn't seem to be quite the place for finches or beautiful thistles. I know it as the place where we grew the big orange mangolds. Council houses were built there in the 1950s. The 'Powers That Be' decided to call the estate Willow Close, but it's still Finches Piece to me!

THE PROMISED LAND

Up on Bredon behind the Big Wood, the Sally Coppice, next to Holcombe Knap, lies a rough undulating field which was called the Promised Land. There is a good reason for its name. When I was a boy, the men of the village told me the sad story.

Early in the century Fred Cormell, who farmed News Farm, had ambitions of becoming a District Councillor. He told a group of young men that they could rent a rough hill enclosure on Bredon to use as allotments on one condition. The condition was that they voted for him at the District Council elections.

Now Doctor Roberson was the sitting Councillor for the District, a respected man to whom many owed their lives and health. It is true also that many in the village owed him money for treatment and medicine, and the threat of him exacting the money weighed heavy on the poor. He always maintained that as long as his patients voted for him at election time he wouldn't press for the money.

Fred Cormell was convinced that he would win the election against the Doctor although another farmer had failed some years before. The result of the poll was a win for the Doctor.

All the previous summer the young men of the Parish had sweated with their hedge hooks, mattocks, forks and spades clearing and cleaning the ground. The smoke from the couch grass fires wafted over the Vale. The land was ready for potatoes and other vegetables. But Fred Cormell, cowed by his defeat by the Doctor, took the land off the men. They called it then the Promised Land; like Moses, it was a land they never possessed.

SPRING HILL

Spring Hill is self-explanatory, a hill full of spring water. One stream runs into a field called the Leasow, now belonging to my nephew. In 1920 villages short of water knew full well about the amount flowing on Spring Hill. A reservoir there, about 600 feet above Tibblestone, would solve their problem. James Cotton, water diviner extraordinary, was a local wise man who used to say he wasn't taken seriously because he had never rubbed his back against a college wall. He contended that the water on Spring Hill, which went underground, was the same stream as in the Leasow. He proved his point by putting permanganate of potash in the spring on Spring Hill and watching the purple-coloured water run into the Leasow.

Parish meetings can be amusing, occasions when men speak their minds regardless. Alf Grove, a respected market gardener, said, 'There's water on Spring Hill in abundance, it just wants harnessing.' Good thinking from an ex-soldier of the Boer War. One chap new to the village had other schemes. Alf looked him up and down before saying the well-remembered words, 'Thee sit down. Thee hasn't been yer long enough to get your seat warm.'

Parish meetings, village-pump politics, are often powerful stuff.

FIDDLERS KNAP

The name of Fiddlers Knap high up on Bredon, over 16 acres of pasture, could be connected to the Whitsuntide sports at Parsons' Folly Tower. Maybe the fiddlers who played when the dancing began were from Fiddlers Knap. Sports such as rough wrestling, or shin kicking for bets were a part of the festivities, along with single sword fencing with staves, and bare-fisted boxing. Side shows such as swing-boats and coconut shies were provided by local showmen. The story of the coconuts being rolled down the hill past the Banbury Stone is just one of Uncle Jim's tales. The stall holder tried to do a Tibblestone man out of his change; but he paid for his crookedness as he watched his coconuts roll down the hill! The workers on the Hill obviously knew their pounds, shillings and pence.

Sadly many of these field names of Tibblestone are being forgotten as hedges are pulled up to accommodate the six-furrow plough and the huge combines. However, towards Beckford a couple of fair-sized fields, Ram Acre and Staits Furlong, are managing to retain their identity. But Hempits, obviously connected in some way with the production of hemp, has been swallowed up by Beckford Way.

Tun Flun, where the cows grazed and where it took half of Mr Bailey's men to catch his iron-grey nag, is a corruption of Ten Furlongs.

What of the Rope Ground? It is about 2 acres on the way to Elmley Castle but still in Tibblestone. The rent money for this land was used by the Church to purchase ropes for the bell ringers. They must have rung with enthusiasm to warrant the yearly rent being put aside for ropes.

There are several fields which belonged to me called Hollbrook or Hollybrook. They are all bounded by a little brook, but why Hollybrook? To be true, there is still one holly tree in the hedgerow, but the association goes a little deeper. Before the threshing machine was introduced in the nineteenth century, corn was threshed with the flail, two sticks jointed with an eel skin. The stick which threshed the corn was made of holly wood, a very hardwearing wood. Two men would endeavour to work in unison when threshing, but it didn't always turn out quite right. Didn't Ralph, out of step, hit Austin Stevens, in his words 'On top of the yud'? Poor Austin.

CHAPTER THREE

BREDON HILL

We cannot concentrate on the Tibblestone Hundred and that part of Bredon Hill without saying something of the Hill itself, that stranded whale which lies between the Cotswolds and the Malverns. It is a limestone hill, oolite limestone ore, a base of Lower Lias clay with Middle and Upper Lias formations in between. The Lower Lias clay is bluish-grey and provides the heavy clay soils of the Vale of Evesham. In fact, the formation extends from the Dorset coast at Lyme Regis to the Yorkshire coast at Redcar. Along the Dorset coast the different strata of rocks are evident in layers of colour from white to brown and red. Excavations on Bredon would unearth these veins of rock and clay. The limestone varies in hardness, as it does on the Cotswolds. Some very soft rock is found on Holcombe Knap, a field half-way up Bredon at Ashton under Hill. By the description of the Hill it means that in the main the top soil is alkaline but at Ashton Wood we find bracken and rhododendrons growing on the Lower Lias, definitely an acid pocket, and there are a few slightly acidic peat bogs around the Hill in which grows the most ancient plant, Fox Tails.

The King and Queen Stones on Bredon Hill, known as Mercury and Minerva, are of inferior oolite carved out of an outcrop of this rock with large veins of quartz running through it. The two main stones are six feet high. Standing a little way south of the main group is a stone of harder rock, a solitary stone yet a part of the outcrop. In between Mercury and Minerva and the solitary stone is a large stone slab covered with moss, at the foot of which is a cluster of small stones. This could have been an altar.

It is probable that these stones were, in the first place, an outcrop on the hill, but what of the stone circle and the faces of Mercury and Minerva? Possibly the Druids worked on these, believing that the stones had fallen from heaven. It is all very interesting, but it points to the fact that there had been intense religious activity by the sun worshippers long before any Christian activity took place.

In her book *By the King and the Queen*, published in 1906, Mrs Jerome Mercier gives a fascinating account of life on Bredon Hill at the time of the Druids.

On Bredon Hill overlooking Bredon's Norton a group of stones, outcrops of limestone, stand like sentinels six feet high looking over the Vale. The two larger ones are known as The King and Queen stones, worshipped by the Druids and the natives of the hill. It was said that they had medicinal properties. A society called The Old People used to dedicate children there passing them naked between the upright stones at the time of the crescent moon. The women stood on one side and men on the other, the child was passed from a woman to the man who blessed it. The words spoken by the old man were:

The strength of the hills, the wisdom of the woods and the bounty of the waters be yours, my son, to the end.

The child it is claimed was given the rite to the power of seeing clearly. It was used as a cure for rickets.

Up until the nineteenth century a court was held there. The King and Queen stones were held in reverence from a period of remote antiquity. The stones were whitewashed when the Court was held but never before asking permission from the King and Queen.

Up on Bredon Hill, that 940 foot outcrop of the Cotswolds, the Druids built their huts, thatched with reeds grown in the Avon Valley. There in the valley the Britons enclosed their cattle on the pastures. The natives lived on meat. They made metheglin or mead from honey and a coarse meal from acorns. Bread was a luxury.

The life of these Druids was bound up with folklore and a mystical belief in nature. They worshipped the sun, they sacrificed animals at their festivals.

Mistletoe on Bredon was an important and sacred parasite growing on the oak trees. At their festivals two bulls were led by youths and as the first rays of the sun came over the Cotswolds the Druid train accompanied by harps and song made its way to an aged oak tree. The Druid on the shoulder of two priests took the golden sickle from the priestess and cut the mistletoe which fell into a white cloth worked with gold held by the priestess. The second Druid cut the throat of the bulls tethered under the oak tree. The carcase was divided, some for the sacrifice, some for the feast here, near the King and Queen Stones, Mercury and Minerva, the patrons of Wisdom.

These festivals were held on Midsummer Eve, on the 1st of May when the mistletoe was cut, and on the last day of October. Fires were lit on the peaks of the Cotswold Hills and Bredon Druids answered with their fire.

The struggle on Bredon came later between the power of the Druids with their sacrifices and the more gentle rule of Rome but the Druids still had a hold on the youth of Britain.

On the hill above Kemerton, an area which was previously part of the Tibblestone Hundred, is an Iron Age camp of 220 acres. Here in the first century BC the Belgae invaded and conquered the natives of the Hill. The invaders must have struck down the folk with such force, as excavations revealed fifty skeletons killed at the final assault on the camp. The natives who survived were forced from the Hill to live in the valley where the Belgae could control them.

This was the last invasion before the Romans came. One positive thing about these fearsome warriors the Belgae was that they were good farmers and they made a plough of sorts to cope with the heavy land of the Avon Valley rather than attempting to farm the poor hill land. The Iron Age camp was excavated in 1935 by Thalassa Cruso Hencken FSA.

J.B. Allies, writing in *Worcestershire Antiquities*, tells how Miss Martin of Bredons Norton was riding her horse along the parapet on top of Bredon Hill in a field called Kemerton Camp early in the nineteenth century. Suddenly, her horse began to sink into the ground but Miss Martin skilfully stayed in the saddle. After sinking some four feet into the landslip, the horse managed to spring onto firm ground. Safe on the firm side of the chasm, which had opened up thirty feet wide and forty feet deep, Miss Martin soon recovered from the fright. Allies states that a vein of black soil was exposed only a few inches under the surface which proved to be decayed wheat; some perfect grains were found in the decayed matter. Speculation has it that this underground granary may have been a cache of wheat, hidden away before some attack on the hill folk. This landslip was near the Banbury Stone, an outcrop of rock near a cave. We know that the Belgae grew wheat in the Vale and may have stored it on the Hill. The natives who lived at the camp didn't grow corn or work the land. The Miss Martin who experienced the awful shock on the Hill was a member of the family that farms a large part of the Hill known today as the Overbury Estate.

The Romans came in AD 43. Beckford, the largest village in the Tibblestone Hundred, stands on a Roman site, which was excavated by Mr Morey Williams in the 1930s. Excavations took place at Nettlebeds and Elmwood above Court Farm. It was here a Roman pottery kiln was found, and broken Roman pottery and coins bearing the names of Roman Emperors are frequently found in the surrounding fields. They date from AD 69 until AD 378, the last date being a few years before the Romans left in AD 409.

The history and folklore that are associated with Bredon Hill may give the impression that it is a 'spooky' place, but if there is a presence there, then we, the folk of the ancient Tibblestone, find it quite the opposite to spooky – a friendly feel, difficult to describe.

Some years ago, as I walked at the edge of night down from the Furze Hill past Canks Bank to the skirting of Ashton Wood, a sort of peace came over me, a sense of well-being. I was not alone but just one of the thousands of my ancestors who had taken that path. The Druids, Iron Age man, the Romans had all passed that way.

The path I took that evening was one that I trod every day, starting from home at 10.30 in the morning, walking up through the little hamlet or cluster of houses known as Paris. I fed a dozen or so calves with cattle cake from the barn. They grazed Paris Hill. From there my journey took me to Parkers Hill above Shaw Green to count some dry cows and see that their water supply was running from the spring at Shaw Green. I walked then through the Leasow up onto Spring Hill, up the gully where the wiry grass and the giant horse mushrooms grew, to Furze Hill. This is where thirty-five store cattle, two-year-old half-bred Hereford heifers, were kept for the summer. It had been a very hot May Day.

Furze Hill is rightly named. The hawthorn bushes are dotted about the pasture, the cattle leaving tracks between a maze of leafy, stunted little trees interspersed with some gorse. The pasture is good between the bushes, and the whole of the bottom of the slope is free of hawthorn. It is a pasture of wild white clover, thyme and fine grass so common on the hills. The thing was that I had already been on Furze Hill earlier on that May Day but – where were the thirty-five cattle? The bree flies were busy, so the frightened beasts sheltered among the hawthorn. I had tried to count them as they dodged me through the maze; thirty-three I made it. Try again; thirty-six. I must have counted one twice. Again I had counted; again only thirty-three. I decided to make tracks towards home, calling at the Kersoe grounds on the way to see that the twelve in-calf Irish Shorthorn keepers were there.

At dinner Dad had said, 'All the cattle alright?'

I'd replied, 'The cattle on Furze Hill were dodging me through the bushes. I'm not sure they are all there.'

'Go up when it's cooler after tea. They will be grazing away from the bushes,' he said.

That is why I was on Furze Hill a second time that May evening. It was an experience. As the path led to what is known as the Blackberry Hill I saw the moon come over the Cotswolds by Broadway Tower. The young rooks had been shot from the elm trees in Great Holbrook and the old birds were crying for their children. It seemed a shame after all the effort the rooks had made building or re-building their homes in March.

In Great Holbrook different shades on the grass on the headland near the stream indicate that a Roman pottery had stood on the site. Here the Romans had plenty of wood for firing and a spring of water. The Irish heifers were all present and there were, sure enough, thirty-five store cattle on Furze Hill. I was never lonely that evening; although I saw no one, I walked with legions of folk who were of the Tibblestone Hundred.

CHAPTER FOUR

MINISTERS OF THE HILL

In 1665 a law was passed that forbade any Nonconformist minister from coming within 5 miles of any corporate town or any place where he had once ministered (except when travelling), nor must he act as a tutor or schoolmaster unless he took the oath of non-resistance and swore not to attempt any alteration in Church or State. This law, known as the Five Mile Act, or the Act of Uniformity, was aimed to deprive the ejected clergy of the means of livelihood by preaching or teaching. The penalty was a fine of £2 or six months in prison.

In 1689 the Five Mile Act was abolished and replaced by the Act of Toleration, although sadly not before thirteen hundred ejected clergy had been imprisoned, with many dying from ill treatment. However, in some ways the Five Mile Act actually spread the influence of Nonconformists in the villages of the Tibblestone Hundred.

From 1665 to 1689 Wood House in Ashton became a sanctuary for Nonconformists as it lay just over 5 miles from Evesham. Here the followers met for religious worship under the wing of some of the ejected clergy. I can picture the worshippers as they trekked from Evesham through Hinton on the Green into the Tibblestone Hundred, on to Netherton and the Saltway, then to Ashton under Hill and Wood House.

The Jacobean Wood House stands as a sentinel over the Vale, facing out towards the Cotswold Edge. Stone-built with stone mullion windows, it is a gem of quality, with floorboards in the bedrooms made of oak planks a foot wide. The deep well in the grounds provides spring water and the wood on the south-west side offers shelter from the prevailing wind. In 1665 the house belonged to Squire Wakeman, the Beckford Lord of the Manor, who was responsible for some of the jurisdiction of parts of Ashton under Hill and Beckford, which in those days formed a single manor. One wonders how the Nonconformists came to have access to such a fine house, but as Wakeman was a Roman Catholic, he too would have been at odds with the Established Church.

This was not the only time that the villages of the Hundred took a religious stance. In *Gloster Notes and Queries* (1884), a monthly chronicle edited by Revd Beaver Blackie, he describes 'The Judgement of Sabbath Breakers'. The story goes that in 1635 Revd William Blackwell, preaching at St Barbara's Church at Ashton under Hill, based his afternoon sermon on 'The Lord's Day', reproving the violation of that day by sports and other activities. As soon as the sermon was done a young man of Ashton under Hill used these words: 'Now that Master Blackwell has finished we will begin.' Taking up the cudgels, the fellow played with them and at the second or third bout he received a thrust in one of his eyes that thrust it out. Thus he was judged.

In 1645 during the Puritan Period Revd Richard Eades succeeded Blackwell as Vicar of Beckford and Paul Griffin became Curate of Ashton. Eades withdrew to Cleeve in 1658 and died at Gretton in 1686. They were known as Presbyterian Intruders.

In *The Good and Great Men of Gloucestershire* (1863), Joseph Stafford states that Eades succeeded Revd Blackwell much later on, in 1663, and that he laboured with much affection and success at Beckford and Ashton under Hill. In 1659, Eades published *The Great Salvation by Jesus Christ*, dedicated to the 'Greatest of Sinners'. Eades' book also contains three epistles which record contemporary issues: one addressed to Rt Hon Lady Veere; the second to Blackwell's sons, Joseph, Jonathan and Isaak; and the third to 'My beloved people the inhabitants of Beckford and Ashton under Hill'. Another item is a contribution by the great Revd Richard Baxter of Kidderminster, a frequent visitor to Eades' two churches. Revd Eades, like many Puritan Ministers, was a Royalist and longed for the restoration of the Monarchy. Lamenting the confusion of the times he exclaimed: 'The whole world is out of order, Church and State. In my prognostic this is English Fate. The land will mourne and men will find it true. Till Caesar comes who will give God His due?' Eades' desires were fulfilled by the return of Charles II to the throne, but he soon found the rule of that most religious prince was intolerable to his conscience.

The Anglican Church was strict about the behaviour of its parishioners. In 1561, Henry Hych of Ashton under Hill was excommunicated from St Barbara's Church, where Thomas Attwood was Vicar, followed by John Chamberlain who was a non-resident minister, for forty days for continuing to deny the power of the Church. Here the dictatorial Anglicans spurned Nonconformity. Peasants were persecuted by the so-called ministers of the God of Love.

On 9 November 1670, a drastic action, known as an Office, was taken by the Church against an Ashton man, William Hicks. It is said that he lay with Ann Jinks of the same parish and that she became pregnant, and he confessed to have had carnal knowledge with her. His punishment was to do public penance in a white robe in the market-place at Tewkesbury the next Wednesday, and the following Saturday in the market-place at Winchcombe, and on Sunday at the parish church, Tewkesbury. He is recorded as saying, in a penitent manner, 'Whereas I have offended God and I am sorry for it, and I agree to certify at the next court'.

One wonders how the religious leaders of the day dealt with other events, which would have been very much community issues. In *Gloster Notes and Queries* (1884), an item is recorded under the heading 'A Great Mortality at Ashton under Hill':

On about May 5th we had accounts from Gloucestershire and other parts of the country that a great number of people died there suddenly of swellings of the throat and other destempers and particularly that they had buried in the village of Ashton under Hill forty five persons since Christmas last out of the inhabitants which did not exceed 100 and those were found to be more than had died in that place in twenty years past.

The last public hanging in Evesham took place in 1744 at Gallows Lane at the top of Green Hill. It is recorded in May's *History of Evesham,* published in the nineteenth century:

In August 1744 a Beckford girl named Elizabeth Owen, who had married an Evesham maltster named Moreton, was hanged, drawn and quartered and burnt on Green Hill, Evesham, for murdering her husband. She came from respectable parents and bought poison from an apothecary's shop in Evesham. She was committed to Worcester Castle and sentenced to death. Friends often visited her and took great pains to console her of the danger she was in unless prevented by a serious and speedy repentance.

She was taken from Worcester Castle at 4 a.m. and conducted by sufficient guard to the place of execution, Gallows Lane, Green Hill, Evesham. When she arrived she was disordered and confused but coming to herself said several short prayers, confessed and died in peace with this world and hoped for mercy in the next. Moreton was not on the Church roll and was probably a Dissenter.

CHAPTER FIVE

DEACKLE'S CHARITY

A BLUECOAT SCHOLAR

John Deackle of Bengeworth, near Evesham, died in 1709 and left money to build a school for the poor boys of Bengeworth. The Deackle School was built in Port Street in Evesham. It was a Bluecoat School and the pupils were dressed rather smartly in bright yellow stockings and quality blue coats. When the school ceased to exist in its own right, it continued under Prince Henry's Grammar School, and was administered by the Governors and the Town Clerk, who provided free places for poor Bengeworth boys.

I remember Deackle Charity pupils at the Grammar School in the 1920s. These privileged few were also given grants for sports equipment, uniform, and so on, and were but a few of the many who benefited from John Deackle's Charity.

My old friend Alf Baker attended the Deackle's Charity School towards the end of the last century. He did come from a poor Bengeworth family, and used to tell me stories of that part of Evesham in that era.

At the Relief of Mafeking during the Boer War, Alf blacked his face and sang at people's doors, a sort of black and white minstrel show, begging from the town folk, who were in a good mood, elated by the victory in Africa.

After his education at the Bluecoat School Alf joined the Salvation Army, becoming a proficient trombone player.

He told me stories of band practices, such as when he got in trouble with the band master for playing an extra note in one musical item. It was where a fly had soiled the music, but Alf was a natural comedian and couldn't help having a joke.

Alf's day-to-day job was in the market gardens of the Vale, and he had a holding on the clay land in sight of Bredon Hill. I knew him as a fairly successful grower. He even developed his own strain of Brussels sprouts. He said he sold to all parts of England.

In 1914 Alf joined the army, and saw service in France. At the end of the war he suffered during that awful flu epidemic. He told me how he was given up for dead, ready to be buried in France, but how he recovered to live to eighty-eight years of age. At eighty-six he still drove his Fordson tractor on spade lugs, ploughing, cultivating that heavy soil, growing his crops for market.

On one of my visits it had been arranged for Alf to do a broadcast about life on the land at the turn of the century. The broadcast went quite well, and then the lady interviewer asked if she could record the sound of Alf's tractor at full throttle, and then hear it stop. She asked him to start it and the 86-year-old, swinging at the starting handle, told her that his language may be a little rough. As the tractor answered with puffs of smoke and the usual coughs of a paraffin tractor, Alf turned and had a minute's blowings, saying, 'Jesus Christ went to Jerusalem riding on a donkey; if he had to have gone on this thing he would never have arrived there.'

Turning to his iron steed he said, 'Come on now old girl'; it started and off went Alf, with a cultivator turning over the heavy clay clods.

We went back to Alf's house for a cup of tea. Alf brought out his precious trombone and played so beautifully *Moonlight and Roses*. He was due to play in a band the following Sunday.

When Christmas came Alf rode his bike to places he knew around the Vale, but was disappointed to find the pub where he had planned to have his Christmas dinner was closed. Returning home to his market garden, he had two sausages for Christmas dinner, but said to me how things would be different next year. I asked him why.

'Well,' he replied, 'I'm having three sausages.'

I wonder how Alf survived, working as hard as he had, but his determination was second to none.

'Ah, Fred lad,' he once said, 'times were hard, but I enjoyed playing in the Army Band with thee Father, he was pretty good on the euphonium.'

When Alf died in hospital the staff told me that he had been calling my name all night long. At the funeral the crematorium chapel was full, not of villagers and local market gardeners but with gipsies who camped on his land, Alf's friends, all dressed in black suits carrying large bunches of flowers. It was a fond farewell to one of the Bluecoat Scholars.

LITTLE SAMMY

As well as providing money for that school, way back in the 1700s, John Deackle also left an endowment of £2,000, which, with interest, amounted to £3,341 in 1743, and this money was invested. In 1749 part of the stock was sold and used to buy an estate of 85 acres at Ashton under Hill. In 1774, under the Inclosure Act, Sir John Rushout, acting for the charity, acquired another 82 acres, making a farm of 167 acres. The farm was situated mainly on the slopes of Bredon Hill, apart from some fields by Carrants Brook which were known as the Needlelands. The rent received in 1774 was £165, almost £1 per acre. By 1830 the estate, let to three tenants, realized £251.

The land on the hill was sold in the 1920s, and the rather splendid farm house known as Walnut Tree House, with a sundial over the gate, was converted into two dwellings. At this time Walnut Tree Farm, Deackle's Charity Farm, was tenanted by Mr and Mrs Kimpton. It was here that their daughter, Margaret, kept a Dames School, and this was where my sister started her education. Margaret and her mother were good, loving, Church folk. I often wondered why Margaret never married; she was beautiful in my schoolboy eyes. Mr Kimpton, a retired bank manager, fetched his morning paper from the station, a walk of a mile and a half. He was a gentleman, with a tobacco-stained walrus moustache, always immaculately dressed with spats over his buttoned-up boots. He walked with a gold-tipped walking stick.

After Mr Kimpton left Walnut Tree Farm a little man, known as Sammy, from the Midlands, and his wife took the tenancy, keeping pigs in the orchard and sheep on the hill. Even though he was a pig farmer Sammy ate neither bacon nor pork, flogging his own bacon coupons during the war.

When his wife died, Sammy found life hard; he was so dependent on her. Making a cup of tea or lighting the oil lamp were things he had never done.

During the war years Sammy helped out on my farm. He was so inquisitive, wanting to know how much my lambs made at market, and how many pots of apples we picked in the cross barn orchard.

Sammy was one of those characters it was hard not to tease. A chap who worked for me put a pound on a local horse at Stratford Races at 5-1. Sammy was anxious to know how much he had won that day as we thrashed a wheat rick. Someone told him it was hundreds of pounds. Roy, who won the fiver, said he would not come back after dinner because he was now so rich.

'What will you do with all that money?' little Sammy asked him.

'Well, I'm having a drinking session for a start,' Roy said.

'I credited you with more sense,' Sammy replied.

'Well,' Roy said, 'That's the answer you get for being so nosy.'

When we sang the hymn at Chapel with the line 'Give me Samuel's ear' and Sammy was seated in front of me, I always felt very tempted to give a pinch or a tweak. On holiday I sent him a postcard from the seaside, forgetting to put a stamp on it. Sammy paid the extra for the postage, but he always maintained I did it on purpose. Poor Sammy!

Sammy ended his life in an old people's home, still asking me when I visited him how much my lambs made at market, how many cattle I had in the yard. There was only one problem at the home. Sammy had to stay in a private ward after keeping everyone awake at night as he counted his sheep, calling them: 'Ho, ho, ho.'

The last tenant of Walnut Tree Farm always was a colourful character; a man who refused to grow old, and who died approaching 100 years of age.

CHAPTER SIX

INCLOSURES

The promoters of Inclosure claimed that, among other motives, their main reason for introducing inclosure was to improve the morals of the poor. They described the state of the poor in pre-inclosure days in depressing terms. In looking after a brood of goslings, a few rotten sheep, a skeleton of a cow, a mangy horse, labourers lost less than they would have gained by a day's work, and so grew lazy and acquired a dislike of honest labour.

One can visualize the daily life of the cottager in those days. Living under outcrops of the Cotswolds such as Bredon Hill, Teddington Hill, Oxenton Hill, the folk had access to a very valuable commodity – wood for firing. Gorse grows to profusion on these hills, and the wood from the gorse bushes is ideal for heating bread ovens. On common land it was there for the taking. Being beholden to a landlord, as would happen under an Inclosure system, would mean losing that right. (The villagers of Beckford relied on the coppice near Benedicts Pool, Grafton Firs, for their firewood; it was a source of fuel for the inhabitants there too.

On the top rung of the social ladder before Inclosure were the Lords of the Manor. They were the Earl of Tyrconnel, Lord of the Manor of Ashton under Hill and Grafton, and Henry Wakeman, Lord of the Manor of Beckford and Bengrove. Next came the freeholders, yeoman farmers, tenant farmers, cottagers, squatters and farm servants, men and women who lived in the big houses.

No distinct line can be drawn between the small farmer, whether freeholder or tenant farmer, and the cottager, except to say that the former made their living mainly as farmers, and the latter as labourers. The men who were mainly labourers did have time off to look after their stock on the common and work on their strips of arable land growing wheat for bread-making. The system had its faults; it didn't result in intensive production off the land. But then, it wasn't meant to, the common land, in fact, was referred to as waste – a sort of eighteenth-century Set Aside.

Court Leets were held before and after Inclosure, and were attended by most of the villagers. One which continued long after Inclosure was held at the King and Queen Stones high on Bredon Hill. Another met at The Tibblestone hard by Teddington Hands, the finger-post pointing the five ways. The Court Leet, with the Lord of the Manor as a kind of chairman, decided on the working of the strips of land. These strips are still obvious in the fields in some parts of Gloucestershire and Worcestershire. High-landed pasture in the fields, once arable strips, divided one man's strip from his neighbour. The lands are so high that, standing in the furrow of one strip one can only just see a neighbour on the adjoining land. Some say the sod was thrown up and ploughed in those ridges for the purposes of drainage; others say that by ridging in that manner more area of land was exposed to sun and wind and rain. Funny, too, how the ant hills on those pastures are all on the sunny side of the ridges. Ants must know where the warmth is. Modern machinery has now levelled most of the high-ridged or high-landed fields.

The simple system employed in the working of the strips was: wheat, spring corn, oats, barley or beans, and fallow. In this way the strip holders had to crop their strips according to the rules of the Court Leet. The farm servant could save wages here; no one was doomed to stay on the bottom rung of the ladder.

A cottager with common rights could graze a cow and geese, and had rights to cut fuel, and he could buy or hire strips of land. On Inclosure, although the cottager who forfeited his rights on the common was often allocated half an acre of land, he lost his independence, and his wages were just the same as when he had his common rights. Strips were given up to neighbouring farmers because the cottager could not afford to fence the land. The cottager lost out. Production of the farm land increased at his expense.

On 3 September 1773, at the Red Lion Inn at Beckford, the home of Edward Drinkwater, a meeting was held to carve up the common land of Beckford, Grafton and Ashton under Hill, and other land in the Tibblestone Hundred. The division of the land was complicated, as so many Parishioners had rights to be considered. The Squire and Parson took the main share. Problems arose when these folk, anxious to obtain as much land as they could, dealt with the men who held the strips. There was pressure put on these men to pay for fencing the land against the Squire and Parson. Some of the little men gave up and forfeited their land to neighbours for very little compensation.

Fencing, called mounding in that day and still referred to as such by a few of the old folk today, could be expensive. The term mounding is self-explanatory. First of all a ditch was dug, the soil from the ditch was thrown up on the side of the owner of the ditch into a mound. Hawthorn or quick thorn was then planted on the mound. This practice resulted in the boundary fence or hedge belonging, with the ditch on the neighbour's side, to the man who dug the ditch. Hawthorn, or quick hedges, were planted in abundance at the time of the Inclosures. Other species of shrubs and hedging plants did appear after some years and the hedges which have a numerous variety of hedge plants are said to be from old inclosures.

Tibblestone was unique in the eighteenth century because a fair amount if its Inclosure land is hill land on Bredon Hill. Here the Cotswold type of stone walls divided the fields. So two types of fencing were involved; hedges in the Vale, stone walls on the hill.

On 18 February 1774 the Beckford Award was made. This award concerned Beckford, Grafton, Ashton under Hill and Bengrove, and was for dividing and inclosing the open and common fields. It resulted in various changes.

The Earl of Tyrconnel was Lord of the Manor of Ashton under Hill and Grafton. Henry Wakeman was Lord of the Manor of Beckford and Bengrove. In the division of the land of the four parishes the Earl of Tyrconnel was allocated 134 acres of land on Bredon Hill known as The Lower Leasowe. In the time of Inclosure, this land, now sub-divided, stretched from Great Hill to Ashton Wood, and in the west to Conderton Common. The Parish Quarry on Great Hill is included. Tyrconnel held earlier inclosures but the award made it clear that he would be responsible for fencing against Sir John Ridout's land and land held by Sir Henry Higford. Higford lived at what later was known as News Farm, Ashton under Hill.

Henry Wakeman was allocated The Groaten, land where pottery and coins were unearthed, the remnants of a Roman settlement. The Groaten, known later as Station Road, consisted of 31 acres of land later to be a part of Stanley Farm. It does seem that there were many earlier inclosures bounding on The Groaten, some of the land of Sir John Ridout and the Earl of Tyrconnel, Wakeman was ordered to fence against them.

The Revd Joseph Biddle became the owner of Carrants Field, land adjoining Carrants Brook, 36 acres bordering land previously inclosed by the Earl of Tyrconnel, land on the east by The Didcot inclosures in Dumbleton Parish, on the west old inclosures of Henry Higford and William Martin, and on the south of the Earl of Tyrconnel. Biddle was also allocated 23 acres known as Little Hill and the Cuckoo Pen, and 17 acres at Hailes Acre, land which belonged to the Church until the twentieth century. This land is bounded by the Deans, an earlier inclosure.

It does appear that the Inclosure of Ashton under Hill was not such a drastic step in land ownership as in some parishes because so much of the land had been inclosed prior to 1773.

Some of the local smallholders at the time were Drinkwater, Vale, Eaton, Cotton, Baldwyn, and Hunt. These families held a little land, gardens and orchards. Henry Wakeman and the Earl of Tyrconnel owned two-thirds of the Parishes, a total of 935 acres, old Inclosure being Wakeman's land. Tithes were payable by the smallholders to the Earl of Tyrconnel, Henry Wakeman and the Vicar of Beckford (at that time the Revd Joseph Biddle): to Tyrconnel was due £1 2s 6d; to the Vicar £1 0s 9d; and to Wakeman 2s 2d. It seems a small sum these days, but it was a sizeable amount for those smallholders to pay.

In Grafton 305 acres of old inclosures were divided up. This included the Earl of Tyrconnel having 107 acres, Henry Wakeman 80 acres, William Beckford 85 acres, and William Nind 15 acres.

In Bengrove, one of the hamlets in the Tibblestone Hundred, 122 acres were inclosed, owned by John Baldwyn and others. (The Baldwyn family still owned Bengrove Farm in the 1920s.) Bengrove lies in a hollow below the 200-foot contour on the north side of Oxenton Hill. The settlement appears always to have been small, with only four houses recorded in 1662. The relative prosperity of the inhabitants when they were freeholders in the seventeenth century is evident from the additions made to two of the houses, rubble-facing, stone-mullioned windows and massive stone chimneys.

Bengrove Farm is timber-framed with seventeenth-century additions; it bears the date 1628 and the initials of John Morris. In 1965 the old site at Bengrove had only the two farm houses and a modern cottage with ponds, although there were signs of former dwellings. Bengrove was once the home of Barbara Wilcox, a great agricultural journalist. It is now the home of Mr and Mrs Alec Hopkins.

Bangrove Farm, as distinct from Bengrove Farm, is a T-shaped property, also timber-framed and with extensions, and has a chimney with the date 1658. For many years it was farmed by the Sexty family, who all lived to be a very great age – William Sexty lived to be over a hundred. The family were great breeders of Shire horses, while Lucy Sexty reared turkeys.

Didcot hamlet lies on the lower slopes of Dumbleton Hill. By the seventeenth century it was reduced to a single farm. The hamlet declined after the fields were inclosed by an early inclosure in the late fifteenth century, but it had been large enough to have a chapel, belonging to Tewkesbury Abbey, that survived until the sixteenth century. The chapel stood south east of Didcot Farm where, as late as 1840, there was a small rectangular inclosure between Great and Little Chapel Hay.

CHAPTER SEVEN

OLD MANOR FARM, ASHTON UNDER HILL

The Earl of Tyrconnel was Lord of the Manor at Ashton, as a part of the Beckford Manor, at the time of the Inclosures of 1774 until 1786 when the estate passed to John Blackburn. In 1856 William Baldwyn became Lord of the Manor.

The Baldwyn family name goes back some six hundred years. The family had a great influence over life at Ashton under Hill; it was a good English family, who did so much for the Church and the people. But William Baldwyn was a weak character who became more and more eccentric the older he got. At one time he became reclusive, while at other times he was known as a market spendthrift. However, in some ways the bachelor squire was a happy man, and one can only smile when the exploits of this eccentric are described.

When William made up his mind he wanted something, he was sure to obtain it. Well known at the local markets, he was never out bid when he fancied a horse, or cattle or sheep. Of course the experienced vendor would slip in a bid and force him to put up his own bid. Lots of the horses he bought turned up on Bredon, with neither halter nor collar. He liked to see them about, he said. They were to be fed but never worked.

For all his crafty dealings, Squire Baldwyn farmed with some skill in those days. He bought two steam engines to plough the land and thresh the corn. He referred to them as his Black Horses. He sacked one bailiff saying, 'I don't like the colour of your hair.' It was red, the same as his own!

In Victorian times it was second nature for the working man to touch his cap when the Squire or Parson passed by. Jim Vale, who worked for me when he was in his seventies, was quite shocked when the village cricket team started Sunday Cricket.

'It wouldn't have done in the Squire's time,' he said with a sigh, longing for the past.

Squire Baldwyn had heard, or maybe it was common practice, of a way of preventing swine fever in pigs. There was so much folklore in medicine and veterinary practice in the Squire's time, and the remedy for swine fever, so the Squire thought, was to cut off a bit of the pig's ear, as well as a snippet off its tail.

'Jim,' the Squire said to his under cowman, 'come along with me.' The Squire was holding a carving knife. Jim followed his master to Middle Farm, where several litters of small pigs had been weaned. The Squire caught the first pig.

'Hold him there,' he ordered Jim. He then cut a piece off the pig's ears and its tail. Not just a snippet but a piece.

'I wouldn't cut quite so much as that off them, Gaffer,' Jim said with some hesitation.

'Just shut up, lad, or I'll serve thee the same,' the Squire retorted.

The outcome of this was that word got round, and the Squire was prosecuted for cruelty to animals.

'I'll let folks know that I'm not cruel to animals,' the Squire said to his neighbours in the local market. 'I'm going to have a show of my stock.'

The show was held in a field known as Tun Flun, or Ten Furlongs, opposite Old Manor Farm House. The whole village was invited. Pony-trotting races were held, and whippet races. The whole of the Squire's livestock which could be shown was penned in that field. Cattle pens made from larch poles were erected by Jonathan Bayliss and Jack Hunting. His sheep were kept in hurdled pens. I've been told by folk who were there that day that his livestock were all in prime condition. Beribboned cart horses paraded the field. Food and drink aplenty was the order of the day. Beef and hams were cooked at the farm house and eaten by the guests in a marquee. Jack

Hunting was busy with a yoke and buckets, he told me, carrying cider from the barn to the marquee to quench the thirst of the hundreds who were there that day.

At the gate the Squire gave a piece of cardboard to visitors to enable them to get a drink at the marquee. Jim Archer, a youth of thirteen, held his hand out for a token. The Squire said, 'Thee bisn't old enough.'

The show was a great success and the Squire had made his point, and in an odd sort of way he did care for animals.

'Jim,' he said to this young under cowman, 'These dogs look starved to death.' Starved was a local term for being cold. 'They need some cider. Bring your little barrel along with me and we will give them something to warm them.'

Jim held the dogs and the Squire poured the cider into their open mouths.

'What about Brindy? You'm frightened of him, Jim.' Brindy, a lurcher, was growling at their feet.

Jim didn't admit he was afraid but just said, 'It's taken all my cider, Gaffer.'

'You can fill up your little barrel in the barn, so come with me.'

All along the side of the great barn the hogshead barrels stood full of cider. 'I want you to taste each barrel and tell me what you think of it.'

The Squire turned the tap on the first hogshead and drew some cider into a pint mug. 'Now Jim, how does that taste?'

'Alright, Gaffer.'

From barrel to barrel young Jim tasted the cider. Some he said was good, some not so good, until he didn't quite know what to reply to his master, the drink beginning to muddle his head.

My Uncle Jim, who worked for Squire Baldwyn in the 1880s after leaving school at eleven years old, was employed in the first place crow minding, keeping the crows off the corn crops. For this he received 6d per day. Then he drove the four-horse team as plough boy at 7d a day.

Jim wasn't pleased with 7*d* a day. He went on a sort of unofficial strike, and spent the days blackberrying on Bredon Hill. He walked the 6 miles to Evesham with the fruit and sold the berries to a fruit shop, returning on the train. He earned 2*s* per day after he had paid the train fare. But one day, who should he meet on the train but the Squire, who said, 'Young fella, thee bist a going towards prison as fast as thee canst go.'

The Squire's workmen were getting 10*s* a week and were allowed half a gallon of cider a day, and a gallon at harvest and haymaking. The cowman, shepherd and carters, who tended their animals on Sundays, were provided with breakfast on Sunday mornings. This meal consisted of bread and fat bacon, washed down with yet more cider.

Uncle Jim recalled many amusing little episodes of the Squire's eccentricity. It is said that when he saw the ducks at the pond shovelling up the corn that was given to them he said it wasn't fair for them to shovel up the corn and the hens to peck it up. He sharpened the ducks' beaks to be like hens.

On another occasion, the Squire said, 'We are going to have some fun today with the ducks. Now Young Jim, catch me four ducks off the pond and bring them into the dairy.'

Jim did as he was told while the Squire partly filled the old galvanized bath with port wine. The bath, used for washing and bathing, was kept in the dairy. It was 3 or 4 foot long and quite narrow. The Squire gathered into the dairy his neighbours and friends, if you could call them that, for they were there to get what they could from the man. The ducks were put into the bath of wine and as they swam around bets were laid as to which one would reach the end of the bath first. There is no doubt these so-called neighbours and friends relieved the old man of a large number of sovereigns.

Jim the under cowman, Aaron Allen the shepherd, Judy Vale the carter and Charlie Dance the Squire's groom were called to the dairy later on. 'I'm going to Evesham in the morning, Dance, is there anything you want?'

Dance replied, 'Well Sir, I could do with some soft soap.'

The Squire said, 'Oh, I dare say there's a lot of soft soap used around here. You chaps take the ducks back to the pond and drink that wine in the bath. The mugs are on the table.'

'I suppose we should do what he has ordered,' Jim the under cowman said to his mates. Charlie Dance reckoned that the ducks hadn't harmed the wine so they set to and started drinking. The Squire and his friends went through to the kitchen to drink whiskey and play cards. Jim told me that he and the other farm workers drank wine until sleep took over. They woke half-way through the night, then retired to Charlie Dance's bothy and harness room where he made a pot of tea and gave them bread and cheese.

The Squire was what could be termed 'trigger happy', really dangerous with his gun. Luckily no one got injured.

'Did you hear me shoot last night?' he questioned Uncle Jim when he was a boy.

'No, Sir,' he replied.

'If ever you do you get up, I shall be wanting somebody.'

The Squire used to take the boys on the hill with him at night, shooting at owls or imaginary badgers. They were supposed to pick up the birds but they could never find any.

Some years later Uncle Jim and Austin Stevens, then seventeen years old, were engaged in cleaning out Carrants Brook down in the mud below the level of the bank. The Squire levelled his gun at their hats saying, 'I thought it was a couple of black crows.'

The Back Lane, previously known as Gipsies Lane, is a very crooked road. One day, the Squire informed his men that, 'I'm going to straighten that lane.' With picks and shovels the men did take out some corners but the lane as I know it includes some almost right-angled bends; these remain. The Squire stood with his gun during that day of lane-straightening, warning the men that he would shoot anyone who altered the lane without going straight.

There is an old saying that truth is stranger than fiction. It certainly was one day on the Moat Pond, the fish pond, when the Squire had to be rescued from there. He had taken to the water in a wheel-barrow saying that he was sailing to America as he was fed up with this country. Well, we all feel like that sometimes but not enough to travel across the Atlantic in a wheel-barrow.

Back at the Manor the coal man Spires called with a load of house coal. 'Do you need any coal today, Squire?' he said, standing by his cart.

'No, I don't want any more,' replied the Squire. 'We had to burn the last lot.'

For three years Squire Baldwyn stayed, reclusive, in the Old Manor. He never came out onto his fields. The farm labourers employed by him became used to not seeing the old man around the yards and fields. One bait time, or lunch time, the men were resting from their task of threshing wheat from a rick near the cross barn. They were sitting in the barn eating their bread and cheese, drinking their cider, when the Squire suddenly appeared in the doorway. The steam engine stood still. 'Now then, get those wheels moving,' the Squire ordered Fireman Davies, the engine driver.

He jumped up from his lunch saying, 'Certainly, Sir', opened the valve on his engine and slowly the wheels turned and the belt made the threshing machine come to life. The familiar hum of the threshing drum sounded more, more, more. No sheaves were threshed, the men continued their bait. The Squire, he was happy to see his engine just turning the wheels. He prided himself on what he called his Black Horses, his two steam engines, and fetched the older boys from their lessons at school to come and help him clean and polish these engines.

It was on a threshing day that Uncle Jim finally finished working for the Squire. He and Austin Stevens were each about twenty years old, strong young men. It was their job to carry the two-and-a-quarter hundredweight sacks of wheat from the threshing machine to the granary. No other men on the farm were capable of that job. The Squire employed lots of old men; some came to work walking with two sticks. He used to say, 'I've had the best out of you, now I'm getting the worst.' He had a point about getting everything from the men as he paid most of the rates at the vestry meeting, and these men were entitled to Parish relief at his expense if they were unemployed. By finding them work at least the Squire did get something for his money.

Young Jim Archer and Austin got fed up with having to do the heavy work on 10s a week; the disabled and old men got the same wage. In the evening, when the threshing machine was silent, Jim went to the Old Manor House to see the Squire.

'And what do you want, young fella?'

'We want more money, Gaffer, as we are doing all the work,' Jim replied.

'You are getting more than you deserve now, but I'll tell you what I'll do.'

The Squire left young Jim at the back door, the dairy door, and went into the hall fetching his gun. 'Follow me young fella.'

The Squire took Jim into the room off the hall where he had spent his time as a recluse. 'Now, here's the gun and here's the cartridges.' From his bureau he then counted 100 sovereigns. Jim was nonplussed, never having seen so much money in his life before.

'You can have all this money, Jim, if you will take the gun and shoot Doctor Roberson. He's offended me.'

'I can't do that, Sir. They will hang me,' Jim said and left his employer. He left the village then too, taking a job on the railway in Leicestershire.

As the Squire got older he became quite dangerous with his gun and used to shoot up one of the wide chimneys of the Old Manor at night. Soon after two male nurses came from London to look after him, and they took the shot out of his cartridges.

The two nurses were taking the Squire on one of his afternoon rides along Beckfords Way in a horse and trap when he collapsed and died. Today, my nephew Charles Archer and his wife, Lesley, farm the Old Manor. I wonder whether they ever see the ghost of William Baldwyn in that little room where he spent three years as a recluse.

CHAPTER EIGHT

THE SQUIRES OF OVERBURY

From the Tibblestone, that limestone rock which stands at the crossroads as a sentinel, a little lane leads towards Bredon Hill. It is called Crashmore Lane. In little more than a mile Overbury emerges spick and span, all Cotswold stone. The Court, that handsome residence of the Martin family, sits graciously at the bottom of the village. Its gardens are in keeping with the surrounding cottages and houses.

John Wesley became friendly with the Martin family while they lived at The Court. Once asked what he would like to be doing if his death came overnight, Wesley's reply was that he would dine with his friend Martin of Overbury, say his prayers and put himself in God's hands, then retire to bed and wake up in the Glory. It is true that we have no record of the Martins being Methodists, but John Wesley mixed with all and sundry. He was always welcome at Tewkesbury but had a rough time in Evesham. His only friend there was Beale Cooper.

The Martins were bankers and the bank took their name. Sir Richard Martin, the nineteenth-century Squire, lived until 1916. He was a landowner rather than a farmer, and the lands of the estate were rented by farmers. Sir Richard lived in grand style at The Court, employing a number of gardeners both in the pleasure gardens and in the fruit and vegetable enclosures. He was a good employer, organizing trips to the sea for his workers early in the century, but he was somewhat of an autocrat, a very nineteenth-century trait. But Sir Richard was a Tory and expected his men to support the Conservative Party with their vote, or at least not vote for the opposition.

James Cotton, water-diviner, standing beside the Tibblestone.

Teddington Hands stone finger-post, with Elsie, my wife, beside it. The five fingers point to Tewkesbury, Overbury, Evesham, Stow-on-the-Wold and Cheltenham.

The King and Queen Stones on Bredon Hill.

Park Lane, Beckford, in the Tibblestone Hundred. (Photo by permission of Oxfordshire Photographic Archives, DLA, OCC)

A gypsy caravan near the plum orchards.

Gypsies encamped near the road. (Photo by permission of Gwyn Richards)

Sam, a Gentleman of the Road, who often travelled through the Tibblestone Hundred.

Tetbury Ted at the Plough and Harrow, Ashton under Hill. Ted travelled the roads around the Tibblestone. He is pictured here wearing a traditional countryman's smock.

Harry Bailey with his family and workers outside Old Manor Farm.

Mrs James Cotton on her way to the
baker's shop at Tibblestone in the
nineteenth century.

Beckford Hall, now converted into flats. (Photo by permission of Oxfordshire Photographic Archives, DLA, OCC)

The Village Cross, Ashton under Hill. The cottage still stands but the old barn has been demolished.

Working on the Loop Line.

The coalman, delivering from the Coal Wharfs, at the siding at Ashton under Hill station.

Bell ringers taking a breather outside the belfry.

The interior of Beckford Church, the biggest church in the Tibblestone.

Woollas Hall today. (Photo by permission of Pam Surman)

Miss Hansford Flood on the steps of Woollas Hall. (Photo by permission of Pam Surman)

Mr Pugh the head gardener, with his assistant at the Hall. (Photo by permission of Pam Surman)

One of Miss Flood's housemaids in the gardens of Woollas Hall. (Photo by permission of Pam Surman)

Joe Green the hermit lived near Parsons' Folly. He raided the fish pond at the Hall for carp. (Photo by permission of Mr Green's grandson)

Prize beef cattle back from the Fat Stock Show in the 1920s. (Photo by permission of Gwyn Richards)

Gloucester Cattle Market with the city centre in the background, 1900. (Photo by permission of David Hanks)

Mr Leonard Hone, in breeches, auctioneer at Beckford Market, selling the sheep. (Photo by permission of Mrs Leonard Hone)

The auctioneer's sons in the sheep pens at Beckford Market, with 'Granny' Lucas. (Photo by permission of Mrs Leonard Hone)

Harry Bailey and his family with
one of his wagons.

Mrs Bailey of Old Manor
Farm with her poultry.

Stanley Farm, my birth-place, with Mother, Father and sister, Clarice, 1926.

Thomas William Archer, my brother, of Old Manor Farm, Ashton under Hill.

Tom Archer, my father, as a young man.

Tom Archer with a Hereford heifer at Stanley Farm, 1927.

The shepherd with his flock, on Bredon Hill in the 1920s.

Musto, one of the gardeners, was a Liberal, and he chaired a meeting of the Liberal Party in the village. He had been warned by Sir Richard, who failed to persuade him against doing such a thing, and he was sacked. The local Liberals rallied to his help and bought him a horse and cart to start a coal round. That business was continued by his son until only a few years ago. Later, the Martin family name became Holland Martin because of a marriage between the family and that of Squire Holland of Dumbleton. Squire Holland was the last Liberal MP for Evesham – a case of life turning full circle.

Life on Bredon Hill in the nineteenth century would have been hard, the area a scrub-covered, rabbit-infested wasteland. During the wet year of 1879 thousands of sheep died through liver fluke. The workers on the Martin estate fed the Cotswold and Oxford Down lambs on turnips, attempting to put some heart back into that thin limestone soil.

Another threat came to the farmers of Tibblestone at the turn of the century. Joseph Arch of Barford in Warwickshire was successful in forming the Agricultural Workers Union, succeeding where the Tolpuddle Martyrs had been crushed. A Methodist preacher, Arch saved enough money in a stocking so that he was not beholden to squires or farmers. With £40 saved he bought his own cottage. He worked across the country, hedge-laying by piece work. He formed a relationship with Miss Sparkes, who ran a Dames School on the outskirts of Overbury, and used her cottage as a base to promote the Union, a fact I learned from the late Percy Attwood. Percy farmed both on the hill and in the Vale in Tibblestone, and was wary of Joseph – this Warwickshire hedge-cutter cut no ice with Percy.

Hordes of workers listened to Joseph Arch as this eloquent rustic addressed meetings in Worcestershire and Gloucestershire, but Percy was not worried that his men would start dictating to him regarding wages. He was already paying them well above the local rate, and no doubt the Martin estate was doing the same. But Arch was a colourful character. An old friend of mine heard him address hundreds of men from a farm wagon in the Vale of Evesham. He was supported in his mission to get all men in the Union by the very left wing Countess of Warwick.

Major Cobb became farm bailiff on the Overbury Estate in 1911. Apart from his involvement in farming, Bernard Cobb was a keen naturalist, a rare hobby in those days before the war. He was continually studying the barometer, noting that 5 February 1911 was the coldest day of the year – mind you, the year was only a little over a month old at that point.

During the First World War Major Cobb served in the Army, his farm bailiff position being taken over by H.J. Glynn for the duration. The Major must still have managed to come home on leave at times though; entries in the diary that he kept record events on the Estate such as a shoot at Overbury in 1915:

December 10th, 1915. No shortage of gunpowder at Overbury despite the bitter war in France. The 10th shoot of the season there were bagged 220 pheasants, 42 duck.

On 17 March 1917 Major Cobb recorded that a 'landmark' invention in farming practice had come to Overbury. He noted this auspicious occasion in just three words: 'Motor plough arrived'. The invention was the Fordson tractor, imported to Britain by Henry Ford. Ford's action of equipping British farmers with the tractors enabled them to produce a larger quantity of food stuffs more efficiently. This in turn played an important part against the threat of food shortages; there was a danger during the war that submarines would interfere with shipping and the supply of food from abroad. Folk at the time were very worried about the risk of starvation. The farm house pantries all had a spare sack of flour stored, just in case.

The 1917 Fordson, with iron-cleated wheels, changed the face of the countryside. High on Bredon Hill the thin limestone, thyme-scented pastures, previously walled in and grazed by sheep, grew barley and oats, but oh, the number of broken plough shares as the plough scraped the underlying stone!

But the pattern changed only slowly. For years the two-horse team with the carter had been a part of the rural scene; from the Overbury stables those massive Shire horses with their feathered fetlocks had ploughed the land after the shepherd had finished hitching his sheep on turnips. Ever so slowly the plough turned one furrow over at a time ready for planting oats or barley. But the Estate, always on the ball as far as progress was concerned, had by then bought a two-furrow Cockshutt horse-plough from Canada. Three horses would plough 1½ acres a day on the hill.

After the Armistice in 1918, on 11 January 1919, Major Cobb was demobilized and resumed his position as bailiff. He organized the peace celebrations and bonfire on 19 July 1919. Full employment and maximum production in Britain lasted until 1921. Then corn from abroad began to swamp Britain and farmers were in a bad way; some said Lloyd George had let them down.

Wages on the land had been good during the war, not because of Joseph Arch's efforts, but because the Wages Board fixed the rate. On 29 October 1921 the Estate gave its workers notice of a wage reduction. It seemed a fair way of balancing the books, better than sacking half the men.

The wage in 1921 was 30s per week for fifty-two hours (about 7¼d per hour), and 9d per hour for overtime. The Estate was being run economically, judging by standards in the town. Daddy Wesson managed the land in the Vale going round on a bicycle, there was no Land Rover in those days and even if there was a bicycle was much cheaper. One man high on the hill at Park Farm turned to fruit growing to earn money. Cottagers on the Estate kept pigs in their sties, a great help towards economy. A Pig Club helped cottagers with the feeding of their cottage pig, and ran an insurance scheme, which paid for a vet when the pigs were ill. A pig show was held on 19 September, when Major Cobb judged the cottagers' animals.

It wasn't all gloom on the Estate, the Church Workers went to the Wembley Exhibition on 21 August 1924, and Major Cobb was given a strawberry weighing 2½ ounces, and the school bought a piano.

In July 1927 S.L. Bensusan came to Overbury with his caravan. This Essex author wrote some of the finest books on farming and country life. The Christmas following the writer's arrival, it is recorded that a severe blizzard cut off houses on the Hill. Joe Green, the hermit, lived in a barn near the Folly. He was the custodian of that building, which had been built by Squire Parsons of Kemerton at the end of the eighteenth century. Major Cobb sent a party up onto the Hill to see Joe Green, which returned with the message, reported on 25 December 1927: Joe Green alive and well. No doubt folk on the Estate were concerned about the hermit, who lived on rabbits and bacon from his pig and who made a weekly trip to Kemerton in the Vale for bread. I'm sure the party took him some provisions, and didn't he poach the pool at Woollas Hall for carp on moonlit nights? Joe, a tough, ragged giant of a man, was a feature of life on the Hill.

Life continued on the Overbury Estate, and as the years went by events and happenings were recorded and remembered. In 1928 the Estate workers dredged Kemerton Lower Pool, and stocked it with two hundred young trout. That same year, Miss Sparkes died, the lady who had allowed Joseph Arch to use her cottage. She had outlived Joseph by nine years. Nothing passed by unnoticed, from the Ashchurch rail crash in 1929, to the day the airship R100 flew over – I remember that day well. Then there were the floods of June 1931, when over 2 inches of rain fell in an hour and the water came gushing down the Hill like a river. However, the following month the Estate was able to organize a fruit stall, held at Teddington Hands, near the Tibblestone.

Major Cobb continued his connections with Overbury Estate. In September 1932 he was on Caldy Island when he heard that the water main at Overbury had burst. Back he came, leak hunting this time. The following year Joe Green, the hermit who lived on the Hill, died. He was buried in Cheltenham. The Major recorded more deaths in those years before the outbreak of the Second World War: Miss Flood at Woollas Hall and Zula Woodhul at Bredons Norton, both colourful characters around the Hill.

In those years just before the war the Overbury farms were run by Mr Thurston Holland Martin, a kind of Arthur Young of the 1930s. At this time corn prices were poor and Mr Thurston rented out the land to market gardeners for sprout growing. My father took 20 acres in Crashmore Lane. It seemed a good move. Our land was getting sprout sick and sprouts had never been grown before on the Overbury land.

Sprout growing down Crashmore Lane was a doddle compared with our heavy land. The Estate ploughman, Bert Randall, drove a Standard Fordson tractor, and prepared the land for our sprout crop. I've seen him jump off the foot-plate of his tractor and the tractor and plough, set at such a nicety, continued without a driver up those long furrows. Bert walked behind and made minor adjustments to the plough. The sprouts did well on virgin garden land. Other market gardeners took land adjoining our 20 acres. One man got a bit vocal in the pub saying what money he had made from the Estate, and the following year Mr Thurston put the rent up.

Mr Thurston was a farmer extraordinaire. He studied the market, he was always ahead of the field. Neighbours watched his every move. If the Estate gave up pig keeping, it was time to get out of pigs. I wonder whether he knew how he was watched. Some may have been envious of his knowledge, but I found him a great character.

The pigeons from the woods were a plague one hard winter. The market gardeners employed Charlie Thatcher, with a gun, to keep the pigeons off the sprouts. They came to our patch and I was commissioned, with a 12-bore, to protect our crop, cycling to Crashmore Lane each day with my gun and cartridges. I made a hide under the top hedge and waited, shooting the birds as they settled on top of the stems. Some days I had a dozen, others one or two. The Estate gamekeeper, a man named Bagget, lived in a cottage in the lane, on a corner still called Bagget's Corner today. Every time I shot he appeared from somewhere to see what I'd killed. He protected the partridges when the shoots were held in winter, and the hedges had butts clipped at intervals for the guns.

'What on earth have you got there?' he said to me one day. 'A rifle?'

'No,' I replied, 'it's called a converted rifle, or a mauser.' The gun was a bolt-action 12-bore with a long barrel; it once stopped a pigeon at 70 yards.

That same year Mr Thurston rode in the Grand National. The Estate bred and trained wonderful blood stock. Unfortunately Thurston's horse fell at Beechers Brook, and he broke a collar bone. He came riding past me one day with one arm in a sling. He and his brother were fearless riders.

'Have you seen Bagget?' he said.

'He was here a while ago, Sir. He will come when I shoot.'

Mr Thurston knew, I'm sure, that I wouldn't shoot the partridges.

Then came the war in 1939. Mr Thurston was the representative on the War Agricultural Committee for our village, and I always found him a gentleman in this role. My father represented Hinton on the Green on the same committee.

During the Second World War Italian prisoners of war lived at Cobblers Quar and worked on the land. Other events, personal and of the Estate, were recorded by Major Cobb, still keeping his diary. On 21 April 1943 the Major was married. There were more problems with the water supply that year, the reservoir having only 1 inch of water left in it. As he had done after the First World War, the Major arranged the peace celebrations and bonfire after the Second, which were held on the Hill on 8 May 1945. He recorded celebrations of a family nature in 1948 when Mrs Cobb gave birth to a daughter on 27 August. In 1949 the Major became Vice Chairman of Evesham Rural District Council. My father served with him on the Council, and remembered him as a very kind man.

Thanks to the Major's carefully kept diaries, we are able to learn about or be reminded of some of the day-to-day affairs and events of the community of the Overbury Estate and its squires as it was in days gone by.

CHAPTER NINE

TIBBLESTONE IN
THE NINETEENTH CENTURY

Working on the farm in the nineteenth and early twentieth century meant long hours of hard manual work. This was recognized by writers such as William Marshall. He described breast ploughing as the most slavish work of husbandry. It took two men the whole day to pare off the turf from 1 acre of land. One man and a boy seldom ploughed three-quarters of an acre of land in a day.

At Ashton under Hill in the Tibblestone Hundred the wages on the farm in 1850 were 7s a week, the lowest in the country, along with Suffolk and Wiltshire. These low wages resulted in my grandfather, in the mid-nineteenth century, with other men of the village, leaving the village at haymaking and harvest to find extra work during this busy period. They mowed the hay fields in the Vale of Gloucester, cut the wheat with bagging hooks and pickthanks, for 5s an acre.

It is true that wages were very low, but this was partly compensated for by liberal amounts of cider, provided by the farmers, potatoes and swedes, and rabbits, readily available from the fields. Some workers were able to keep a pig. Marshall, writing about conditions at that time, states that the amount of drink given to the men was shamefully exorbitant. Three quarts a day was a common allowance, frequently two gallons a day, sometimes nine or ten quarts, or an unlimited quantity.

The wagoner or carter was the best paid of the farm labourers. He had to have his plough team out in the fields by 7 o'clock, but to prepare his horses for the day's work he had to be at the stable by half past five and he needed to look after his horses on Sundays.

At harvest time the men rose early from their beds in the farm barns. The farmers provided them with a variety of food and cider. When the men had bread and cheese they chanted: 'Bread and cheese, take your ease.' With ham and eggs they said: 'Ham and eggs, mind your legs.'

I can picture the scene at harvest time: a team of men with scythes circling the hay field with the young mower in front. The idea was to break the young man in by mowing close to his feet and pushing him along. Grandfather used to tell Dad that the art of mowing with a scythe was to keep the knoll or bed of the scythe down, and when they whetted the blade, to put a long edge on so that they were not obliged to stop and sharpen their tool too often.

When small tufts of unmown grass were left in the field it was said with sarcasm that there were a lot of partridge nests in the field. Partridge nests were left undisturbed, with unmown grass around them.

It appears that Tibblestone did not escape the Swing Riots of the mid-nineteenth century. These riots were the result of the labourers' fears that the threshing machine would do them out of work. Threshing by hand, with a flail, would provide employment for the men throughout the winter, but the steam thresher would do the job far more quickly and required fewer men. Ricks and barns were burnt down by the labourers at Dumbleton and over the border at Winchcombe, but in the nearby Cotswolds, by the 1860s, steam threshing was becoming more common.

In the Hundred of Tibblestone the task of ploughing was usually done by one of two ploughs. The Gloucestershire plough, a wooden implement without wheels and pulled by two horses, could plough three-quarters of an acre of land in one day. These ploughs were good for ploughing back fallow land on the heavy clay. The second, more popular plough was Kells Iron Champion plough, which sold at £5 17s 6d in the nineteenth century. I drove the horses pulling one of these ploughs in 1930.

By working long hours and saving hard men could improve their living standards. Grandfather saved enough money in a stocking to buy a Grandfather clock for his wedding for £5. But the price of hard work did have an effect on health. He helped with laying drains in the winter time, working in all weathers, standing in water in the trenches and laying the pipes. In those far-off days before wellington boots, his feet and legs were often wet through. Dad told me how he had seen his father return from work in winter when the frost had frozen his cord trousers onto his legs.

Foreign visitors often give highly dramatized, though not necessarily accurate accounts. One American, touring the West Country in the mid-nineteenth century, thought that the labourers in Gloucestershire were the most degraded, poor, stupid, brutal, licentious that he had seen throughout the country. Worse, he said, than those in Germany and France; men whose tastes were just mere instincts or whose purpose in life was so low, so like that of domestic animals. That is all a matter of opinion.

So the land was worked in the mid-nineteenth century, cultivated with implements from Kells of Gloucester and the village blacksmith. The Cotswold type of land on Bredon was ploughed with oxen. These animals were worked until they were five years old and then fattened for beef. It can be said that beef of that age would be tough but by hanging the sides for a while it would eat quite sweetly.

James Cotton, as a boy, drove the bullocks at plough on Bredon. The stables by Great Hill Barn housed these teams of oxen. One assumed that they were Hereford cattle or Longhorns. During the Crimean War many acres of pasture land in the Tibblestone Hundred were ploughed up. Some of the steep ridges created during that time remain today.

Kells nine-furrow, or nine-row, drill was made in Gloucester and was introduced in 1874 at the Worcester Agricultural Show; although it speeded up the cereal planting, many farmers still stuck to the five-furrow drill, pulled by two horses, or the one-horse, three-furrow drill. On the small farms wheat was dibbled in with setting pins, a few grains in one hole. One for the pigeon, one for the crow, one to rot and one to grow.

The wheat and oats were still cut by hook and by crook but the reaping machine was being used on some farms. The mechanical reaper pulled by three horses cut the corn and delivered it in sheaves which had to be tied by the workers. In the late nineteenth century, this job too was taken over by the mechanical binder. Meats of Cheltenham delivered one machine to a farm at Grafton. It really did become a talking point in the pubs at that time. The farmer was so particular about safety he would send an extra man to the field to sharpen the knife of the binder. He was equipped with a first-aid package in case any one of the three-man team got injured.

With the importation of so much Canadian wheat the farmers of Tibblestone turned to early market gardening for revenue. For centuries the black soil of Evesham had grown crops of vegetables and provided the Midlands with produce. When the railways came in the nineteenth century the area under Bredon became accessible to Birmingham and the North as well.

Some Evesham growers moved to the Tibblestone villages at the end of the nineteenth century. They brought with them the know-how about the production of fruit and vegetables. Among them were Mr Harry Bailey, who came to Ashton under Hill, Wilson Bedenham, who came to Beckford, and James Marshall, who was already growing market garden crops at Ballards Farm, Hinton on the Green.

CHAPTER TEN

THE LOOP LINE

On 9 June 1861 the railway line from Evesham to Ashchurch was authorized. This 10-mile stretch of the line was to become a section of the Barnt Green to Ashchurch branch. The new railway, to run on the eastern side of Bredon Hill, was a bypass to the main line which ran the other side of the Hill. It was planned to join three of the villages in the Tibblestone Hundred, namely Hinton on the Green, Ashton under Hill and Beckford.

Since 1840 the main line between Birmingham and Gloucester railway had been running on the other side of Bredon Hill with a station at Bredon. But the Oxford to Worcester line was bedevilled by a dispute with the contractor, and tunnelling through the Cotswold limestone at Mickleton took six years to complete by the navvies from Wales and the Black Country, while Lord Coventry insisted that Pershore station was built nearly 2 miles from the town at Pinvin.

Squire Baldwyn of Ashton under Hill and Squire Holland of Dumbleton, whose Estate was partly in the Hundred of Tibblestone, were concerned about the prospect of the Loop Line, as the new line was called. They wanted a railway and had cooperated with the surveyors in choosing the route along the Carrant Valley. However, as there were many little railway companies owning or leasing sections of line, how they had to choose who they wanted both to construct and to work the railway round the Hill.

Squire Holland was in favour of the Midland Railway Company working this section going through Tibblestone. He knew Mr Liddle, the Midland engineer, and wrote a letter from his London Club to his solicitor George Badham of Tewkesbury. Squire Holland was concerned about who had the contract for constructing the new railway link. He had doubts about the financial state of a Mr Thomas, who wanted the contract. He was wise when he doubted the power of this contractor to take on the already strong Midland Railway Company, and eventually the Midland Railway appointed Messrs Liddle and Gordon as engineers for the new line.

So the Midland gave us our railway, but not before there were many disputes over the exact route it was to take through Ashton. Joseph New, who farmed the 280-acre farm north of Ashton, agreed to the line cutting through his land on certain conditions. The original proposal had been to build a station at Hinton on the Green and another at Beckford, missing out Ashton under Hill. But Mr New insisted that if the railway came through his land with the line, then a station must be built at Ashton, and one was built. It does seem that landowners in the late nineteenth century still had some voice compared with the compulsory purchase of land for motorways in the twentieth century.

The landowners involved in selling land to the Midland Railway Company were Squire Baldwyn, David Drinkwater, Herbert New, Joseph New and Nehemiah Cole, and a small farm house, rick yard and cattle sheds belonging to Hannah Abel also had to be taken into account.

The solicitor for the Baldwyn Estate was Mr Garrat of Evesham, who concocted a story that he would like to check the Baldwyn deeds. This he did, substituting some useless documents in their place. Using the Squire's deeds as security, he bought Hannah Abel's farm thinking that the house, buildings, and meadows near Carrants Brook would be wanted for the route of the Loop Line. He hoped to sell the lot at a profit to the contractors when they constructed the line.

The surveyors meanwhile were making sure that the railway would not be flooded by Carrants Brook. The route they settled for was on the left of Nehemiah Cole's land at Sandfield and came along the top of Joseph New's Pecked Meadow, then along west of the Naits, a pasture field that flooded in the winter. Hannah Abel's farm was left 484 yards east of the proposed line and Mr Garrat was left with a much less valuable house and holding than he had expected. Indeed, his calculations were so wrong that he went bankrupt. When the Bankruptcy Court heard the case, the truth came out about his fraud.

It was sad that the Baldwyn Estate had been robbed by this solicitor they trusted. The Squire proposed taking Hannah Abel's farm as payment for his loss but, as Garrat was already bankrupt and paid his creditors 6d in the pound, the Baldwyn Estate lost over £6,000 through Garrat's fraud. Garrat went to prison for this, but it was no real consolation to Squire Baldwyn.

As today, the odd protest at anything new came from a few villagers, Walter Peart in particular. Walter was opposed to the new line. He told the Squire one day on the Hill, as he penned his ewes, ''Tis no good, Master. Spoiling the best haymaking meadows by Carrants Brook. We don't need a railway, it's only five miles to Ashchurch and the main line.'

Walter came to the village from Somerset as shepherd to the Squire. He added, 'Now when I was in Zummerset years ago I did walk scores of miles over the Mendips.'

On 1 October 1864 the new line was opened to both passenger and goods traffic. Squire Baldwyn and David Drinkwater organized a great feast in The Groaten, afterwards known as Station Road. Charlie Dance, the Squire's groom, organized horse races over jumps in The Groaten field. The field was marked out for races for the boys and girls. Union Jacks hung from larch poles, trestle tables were weighed down with great joints of beef and pork from fat pigs. Dinner was held at one o'clock, then came the races, followed by horse jumping by local farmers, dog races and a parade of the fox hounds. When the cider was running low and the bonfire lit up the sports field, Squire Baldwyn presented Joseph New with a Georgian silver tankard with this inscription:

Presented to Joseph New of Ashton under Hill by his friends and neighbours for his successful exertions in obtaining a Railway Station in the Parish. 1864.

The Squire and David Drinkwater were concerned about how their horses would react to the steam and smoke from the railway engines as they crossed the bridges of The Groaten and Gipsies Lane. Alongside the track their men were now busy erecting fences in the long paddocks where the horses were put to graze close by the trains. Oh, they reacted at first when the ground shook as the heavy black engines belched steam and smoke, but after a while the horses took little notice of their new iron neighbours. This prepared them well for when they pulled the wagons and carts taking produce from the land to the trucks in the sidings.

In the course of constructing the railway sand and gravel had to be hauled from Rabbit Lane at Beckford, and the old road known as Beckfords Way did get damaged by the heavy wagons and carts. A Vestry Meeting was called on 24 March 1865, at St Barbara's Church, Ashton under Hill. The minutes of the meeting were worded as follows:

Whereas at a Parish Vestry Meeting held on the above date the purpose of which is to consider the damage done in the transition of materials through our Parish for the necessary appliance in the construction of yards and approaches at Ashton Station near here, We estimate the damage at the sum of £160.

Persons Present.
David Drinkwater.   Church Warden.
John Hemming.   Church Warden.
Joseph New.   Way Warden.
Thomas Baldwyn.   Way Warden.
William Baldwyn.   Chairman.

Rev: Joseph Harrison.

So the Midland Railway Loop Line was established and soon the station became a hive of activity. A coal wharf was started, railway trucks were loaded with corn and fruit from the farms for faraway towns and cities. Passengers travelled to towns they had heard of but never seen before.

One Ashton man, who worked at Beckford 2 miles away and had always walked home in the evening, decided to take the train instead and arrived at Ashton station with his ticket. The porter in charge said, 'Tickets please.'

Jonathan replied, 'I've paid for this bit of paste board, I'm keeping it, it's mine.'

Another rather cheeky porter, when asked by the Squire, 'How long will the train be?' replied, 'Not quite as long as the platform, Sir.'

The villages of Tibblestone Hundred, Beckford, Ashton under Hill and Hinton on the Green, were well served by the Loop Line, which, as it were, opened up the world to them. But the line also served the adjoining village of Elmley Castle, Hinton on the Green being its nearest station. Sedgeberrow folk went to Ashton under Hill for railway journeys, while Beckford, with its goods yard and other amenities, catered for neighbouring villages as well.

Soon excursion trains were running to Sharpness in Gloucestershire, connecting with a steamer which took working men, men who had never seen the sea, on trips to Ilfracombe. Some went to Scarborough and fell asleep on the train, ending up in Newcastle. Some, more adventurous, went on trips to Cherbourg. The train altered the pattern of life for many: town and country folk became near neighbours.

There were, of course, one or two who complained. One farmer from Tibblestone who fed Hereford-cross cattle for beef on his 250 acres had a rick fire one summer. It was a big rick near the railway. He blamed the sparks from the engines, but Fred Cormell, that cute stock breeder of News Farm, was under suspicion. Fred was complaining about the loss of the hay to Dinky Roberts, the one-armed farmer of the Old Manor.

'Well Fred,' Dinky Roberts said, 'your hay rick, a pity I know, but when you get home just have a look in the looking-glass and you will see the man who set fire to your hay rick.'

The Loop Line not only brought benefits to the villages under Bredon Hill but also to the North Cotswolds. Places like Winchcombe, Toddington, Stanway, and so on, could now collect their coal from Beckford station. (There was no station at Winchcombe itself for another forty years.)

With its station, Beckford became a Mecca. To be true the village already offered a lot of facilities. A Petty Sessions was held at Court House, and the village had a Sergeant of Police and two Constables. The post office was able to issue dog and gun licences, and the inn had a spirit licence!

Archdeacon Timbrell was responsible for Beckford having coal gas lighting when the railway came and the coal wharf had been completed at the station. A miniature gas works, with an operator living in Gas Cottage, supplied gas to Beckford Hall, the adjoining cottages, the Church and the Vicarage. It was quite fantastic that, in this backwater of Gloucestershire, the parishioners had this benefit way back in 1866.

Revd Timbrell had put up £400 for this amenity. But the station was a new focal point for folk and goods. A large building housed the stacks of produce to be delivered by horse and dray to the Hundred villages and to Winchcombe. Mr Hulse of Ashton under Hill saw the prospect of a good living hauling produce from Beckford, transporting the loads of sugar, flour, tea, and other commodities to the grocery shops at Winchcombe and elsewhere. Mr Hulse worked with a number of drays, employing five or six carters. He lived at Charity Farm way up on Bredon, known as Parkers Hill. Ralph Pratt was in charge of the horses and he brought them down Cottons Lane every morning very early, nose to tail in a sort of convoy. Some were used as trace horses to help the shaft horse to haul heavy loads such as coal up Stanway Hill. At Charity Farm Ralph fed and watered the team, groomed them ready for the dray men to arrive at 7 o'clock.

On the Toddington Estate, just outside the Tibblestone boundary, there had been planted the largest acreage of fruit ever attempted in England, with a jam factory to process some of the produce. During the season Mr Hulse's drays hauled plums, apples, pears, and loaded the fruit at Beckford station. The drays took load after load to Beckford to be transported all over Britain.

Beckford was surely an important place after the railway came. No wonder the saying was, when some village chap got a bit above himself, 'Thee hast been to Beckford.'

CHAPTER ELEVEN

WOOLLAS HALL

Just over the border into Worcestershire, adjoining the Tibblestone Hundred, John Hansford rebuilt Woollas Hall in 1611 on the site of an older house. Part of the old house was retained to form kitchens and servants' quarters. The new house included a baronial hall complete with minstrels' gallery and stained glass windows. Above the open stone fireplace was placed the Hansford Coat of Arms, above a Latin inscription which translated read 'Beware of thy end'. One interesting feature of the house was the priest hole, where priests used to hide during the Civil War. The priest hole was behind a wide fireplace in the baronial hall; once the priest was safely hidden a fire was lit which concealed the entrance. Nearby was another curious detail – a never-failing spring which provided water for the house. It bubbled up between the flag stones near the priest hole. Any overflow was piped down the hill to a pool where the water-lilies grew and the carp multiplied.

A Jacobean staircase sweeps to the top of the house, leading to panelled bedrooms. At the top is a chapel where the Hansford family worshipped. John Hansford died five years after building the hall.

In 1679 Compton Hansford was Lord of the Manor and Master of the Hall. His wife was a second cousin of Lady Winter. Two members of the Winter family had been involved in the Gun Powder Plot of 1606 and had been hanged, drawn and quartered.

Early in the nineteenth century the Estate passed to Edward Hansford. Edward married Elizabeth, daughter of James Martin of Overbury who was MP for Tewkesbury.

In 1854 Edward and Elizabeth's son, John, inherited the Estate. He died in 1860, unmarried, and left everything to his sister, Frances, wife of William Lloyd Flood of Flood Hall, County Kerry. The last of the family line was Anne Hansford Flood, godmother to John Masefield. Hers is an interesting story.

Anne Hansford Flood, the last of a long line of Bredon Hill landlords and ladies, lived alone at Woollas Hall. This distinguished lady loved her garden, bought plants at Chelsea Flower Show, planted them in the greenhouse. However, her under-gardener, Brown, was rather too enthusiastic in ridding the borders of weeds.

'Where is that blue convolvulus, Pugh. The Morning Glory? I asked you to plant it under my window.'

'So I did, Ma'am, isn't it growing?' Fred Pugh replied. 'I'll fetch Brown to see you Ma'am, he's our under-gardener.'

'Now Brown, where is that plant?'

'I thought it was bindweed, Ma'am, so I dug it up and put it in the incinerator.'

'Thank you, Brown, for being truthful,' Anne replied.

No more was said and no doubt Brown was more careful afterwards.

As often happens in a situation where a maiden lady lives alone in a large house with a baronial hall, the butler takes on the duties of the Master of the House. McGuire, the Irish butler at the hall, was no exception. He had a close relationship with the cook; both of them being Catholics they attended Mass together on Sundays, across the hill at the Catholic church in Kemerton. It was a day in early autumn, a bright, sunny day, after harvest. Being Sunday, McGuire and the cook walked to Mass leaving the young servant girl and the footman, Jack Wool, in the house to prepare the dinner. The servant girl had been ordered to boil beetroot as one of the vegetables for the meal.

Returning from Mass, McGuire discovered that the girl had pricked the beetroot with a fork, bleeding it until it was almost white. In a rage he threatened to sack her. He beat her around the kitchen with a rolling pin. She ran down the hill in terror.

'Where is the kitchen maid?' Miss Flood inquired in the afternoon.

'She ran away. I scolded her for bleeding the beetroot.'

'McGuire,' Miss Flood said sharply, 'you know I can never keep maids as long as you are so strict with them. You find her and bring her to me.'

McGuire, the cook and Jack Wool searched the gardens, the greenhouse, the stables, but there was no sign of the servant girl. It was getting dark when the footman found the poor girl floating among the water-lilies on the pond. Sadly Miss Flood helped to lay her on her bed in the servants' quarters while the footman fetched the doctor from Tewkesbury in the pony and trap. Jack was so upset, for he was fond of the girl and he had tried to protect her from McGuire's anger. After the funeral at Eckington his feeling of anger at the death of the girl generated into a quarrel between himself and McGuire.

A week later Miss Flood called for her butler. She called in the great hall, in the pantry, but got no reply. She and the cook searched the house but never found him. However, they did find Jack lying in the priest hole, bleeding from a stab wound. Fortunately, the good doctor saved his life. As for McGuire, he was never found. He had returned to Ireland in a hurry and was never seen again.

Miss Flood never replaced the butler, and managed to run the hall for the rest of her days with her footman. Although Jack was a loyal servant, he was also superstitious to the extreme, a dreamer, a dabbler in Black Magic. He and the cook held sessions in the Folly Tower on the night of the full moon. Joe, the hermit who lived in a barn by the tower, spied them from his lodging, saw a black retriever dog sacrificed, heard the oaths made, the Lord's Prayer repeated backwards. On those nights of the full moon Joe stayed up and dressed, ready for anything, and when the cook and the footman walked past the Banbury Stone to the hall Joe sat by his fire reading from the great brass-buckled Family Bible.

Up in the chapel at the top of the hall, in a kind of cage, stood a statue in stone, a fearsome gargoyle of a man carved from the

Bredon Rock at the time of the Gun Powder Plot when the hall was a refuge for Catholics. It was late on Sunday night when Miss Flood found her footman and cook kneeling in front of the statue.

'What are you doing, are you worshipping idols? Leave the chapel at once.' These words from Miss Flood ended that evening's session in the chapel.

Next morning Miss Flood called Pugh, the gardener, to her room. She explained the evening's happenings, seeking his advice.

'I'd remove it if I were you Ma'am,' Pugh said quietly as if the walls would hear.

'Yes, Pugh. I am glad you think that way, for I would like you to smash it with a sledge hammer, break the stone to pieces and use it to repair the drive.'

'Yes, Ma'am,' Pugh replied and did her bidding.

'Another thing, Pugh,' Miss Flood said quite sharply. 'I have a suspicion that our cook is in the family way. Do you know anything about this, Pugh?'

'Not surprised,' Pugh replied. 'I reckon I could name the man but you know Ma'am, it's none of my business, and the cook has played with more than one on the Hill.'

'Come, come, Pugh. You must tell me, our cook comes from a Convent, it is most irregular.'

'Now Jarvie Partridge, the gamekeeper has been seen with her. But if I have to name the man 'tis McGuire, as fled to Ireland.'

'How can you be sure Pugh? Tell me.'

'Well, Ma'am, if I'm to be blunt and straight to the point, I've seen him riding her on Sunday mornings in Battens Wood after Mass.'

Anne Flood blushed a little, then smiled. 'Oh, Pugh,' she replied, 'you are so much a part of the Hill, your descriptions are so direct. Thank you. I'll have a word with our cook.'

The cook admitted that McGuire was the father of the child she carried. Miss Flood promised to keep her at the hall, having compassion for her because of the way she had been treated by the old butler.

Weeks passed, months passed, no one quite knew when the cook's baby was due. A cold frost on a late winter's morning on the Hill gripped the earth. The recent fall of snow lay solid over the fields. As Joe, the hermit, lit his fire, then fetched water from the spring, he noticed patterns of rabbits' footmarks faint on the frozen hill. Jarvie Partridge rode his forest pony from Cobblers Lane above Beckford with a bottle of home-made wine to share with the hermit.

Suddenly Pugh the gardener ran from the hall past the Folly Tower calling, 'Jarvie, can you help?' As he came closer he said, 'Quick, Jarvie. Can you fetch the doctor to the cook.'

Jarvie didn't ask questions, he knew the trouble Miss Flood had with her cook. He rode his pony to Bell's Castle. Doctor Overthrow was just leaving on his rounds, untying Lavender, his horse, from the railings and mounting his high trap.

'Doctor,' Jarvie called. 'Can you come quick to the hall, the cook's being confined.'

Doctor Overthrow immediately drove Lavender furiously along the old coach road to the Vale. At the hall the cook was lying on Miss Flood's bed propped up by pillows, stone hot water bottles at her feet, crying with pain. Anne Flood stood by the bedside with smelling salts, which she offered to the cook every time a spasm came on.

'Carry her to the dining table and put blankets under her.' The Doctor's gruff stern orders were obeyed. Martha, the maid, and the footman obliged.

''Tis serious, devilish serious.' Those words from Doctor Overthrow made Miss Flood and Martha wince.

'No ordinary confinement. I'll have to operate now,' the Doctor said as he took bottles of anaesthetic and instruments from his bag. 'The cook has conceived in the Fallopian tubes. I'll have to take the baby from her.'

The Doctor worked and sweated for a while until the operation was complete. He saved the cook's life but the baby was dead. Jarvie's ride to Bell's Castle to catch Doctor Overthrow had been vital, otherwise the cook too would have died. Perhaps he felt obliged, for he had found pleasure in the cook's company more than once. Jarvie was a complex character. A great wit, a sage of sorts, but no one ever got to the bottom of his thinking, not even his tight-lipped, lean wife.

Nothing at Woollas Hall ever had any pattern of normality to it, including the antics of the staff. The cook remained, but the goings on with the footman worried Miss Flood. Their sessions of Black Magic were now held at the Banbury Stone below the Tower. Joe witnessed many things there.

Miss Flood gardened, working with Pugh and growing prize dahlias. Visitors often mistook her for a gipsy lady, for in the garden she wore a cotton bonnet, a sacking apron over a blue frock, and boots buttoned up to her slender calves. Anne Flood was mistress of the hall, the flat land of Bredon Hill, the Parsons' Folly Tower, the workmen's cottages which formed a rough oblong on the escarpment of the stranded whale-shaped hill of 1,000 feet.

Pugh was taken into her confidence now McGuire had fled to Ireland. Maybe Jack Wool would have been her right-hand man, but Miss Flood was dubious about his association with her cook and the mystical union between them. Joe knew of the macabre antics of his neighbours, but these many secrets were buried with him on 28 February 1934. Miss Flood died in her bedroom at the hall in 1936.

William Cobbet provides a detailed description of Woollas Hall in *Rural Rides*, first published in 1830:

I went to see Mr Hansford at his house and estate at Bredon Hill which, I believe, is one of the highest in England. The ridge, or rather the edge of it, divides, in this part, Worcestershire from Gloucestershire. At the very highest part of it there are the remains of an escarpment, or rather I should think, a citadel. In many instances in Wiltshire, these marks of fortifications are called castles still; and, doubtless, there were once castles on these spots. From Bredon Hill you see into nine or ten counties; and those curious bubblings up, the Malvern

Hills, are right before you, and only ten miles distance as the crow flies.

As this hill looks over the counties of Worcester, Gloucester, Hereford and part of Warwick and the rich part of Stafford; and, as it looks over the Vale of Evesham, Worcester, and Gloucester, having the Avon and Severn, winding down them, you certainly see from Bredon Hill one of the richest spots in England, and I am convinced, a richer spot than is to be seen in any country in the world; Scotland excepted.

The Avon falls into the Severn just below Tewkesbury. Mr Hansford's house is on the side of Bredon Hill; about a third of the way up, and is a very delightful place.

The house is of ancient date, and it appears to have always been inhabited and the property of the Roman Catholics; for there is, in one corner of the very top of the building, up in the very roof of it, a Catholic Chapel, twenty-five feet by ten feet. It has arch-work, to imitate the roof of a Church. At the back of the Altar there is a little room, which you enter through a door going out of the Chapel; and adjoining this room, there is a closet, in which is a trap door made to let the priest down into one of those hiding places, which were contrived for the purpose of evading the grasp of those greedy Scottish minions, to whom that pious and tolerant Protestant James 1st delivered over those English gentlemen who remained faithful to the religion of their fathers, and, to set his country free from which greedy and cruel grasp, that honest Englishman Guy Fawkes, wished, as he bravely told the King and his Scottish Council, 'to blow the Scotch beggars back to their mountains again'. Even this King has, in his works had the justice to call him 'the English Scaevola' and we Englishmen, fools set on by knaves, have the folly, or the baseness, to burn his effigy on the 5th November, the anniversary of his intended exploit. In the hall of this house is the portrait of Sir Thomas Winter, who was one of the accomplices of Fawkes, and who was killed in the fight with the Sheriff and his party. There is also the portrait of his lady who must have spent half her lifetime in working on some very curious sacerdotal vestments, which are preserved here with care, and are as fresh and as beautiful as they were the day they were finished.

Cobbet, you will admit, waxed lyrical of Bredon Hill and his description of Woollas Hall. He speaks of Leicester sheep on the Hill which surprises me so near to the home of the Cotswold breed. When Cobbet says that nine or ten counties can be seen I wonder whether he climbed with Squire Hansford up the 40-foot tower, Parsons' Folly. Built by Squire Parsons in about 1795 to make a mountain out of a hill, the tower raised the height from 960 feet to 1,000 feet. I wonder.

CHAPTER TWELVE

The Lords of the Manor of Ashton under Hill

Squire William Baldwyn became Lord of the Manor of Ashton under Hill in 1856. The Baldwyn family had been landowners for hundreds of years but never claimed the title of Lord of the Manor at Ashton, just the Squire. The Wakemans of Beckford had held a claim of the Ashton land, and John and Edward Blackman held the Manor before Squire William Baldwyn.

I have described the sometimes rather strange antics of Squire William Baldwyn in other places, mostly stories told by Uncle Jim who worked for him. But despite his strange behaviour I often think that life under Squire Baldwyn was much better than life under many other landowners, and that perhaps the farm workers took advantage of him towards the end, as an ageing Squire with some rather eccentric ways. William Baldwyn died in 1899, and it seems a shame that there was no other member of this illustrious family, a family which included the later Stanley Baldwyn of Bewdley, to continue working the Old Manor Farm.

In 1902, three years after William Baldwyn's death, the farm was bought by John Collins of Evesham and Broadway. He became Lord of the Manor with the manorial rights, but he never actually lived at the manor house. One assumes that he purchased the property at a reasonable price purely as a speculation.

Collins and his sons were butchers, and had shops in Evesham and Broadway. They were top grade men in the trade. One son, Frank, farmed the Middle Farm at Ashton under Hill, land which stretched from the village to the station and beyond.

John Collins sold the Old Manor to Arthur Roberts in 1906, retaining Stanley Farm and Middle Farm where Frank lived. Stanley Farm was let to Thomas Bury. He had been a tenant under Squire Baldwyn but Thomas Collins, John's son, gave him notice to quit on 29 September 1900. No reason was given. Arthur Roberts farmed 4 miles away at Great Washbourne where he lived, He never occupied the Manor Farm House. Arthur was a shrewd man, who had the nickname Dinky Roberts. Some years before coming to farm at the Manor Arthur had an accident with a chaff cutter and lost his arm. The name Dinky stemmed from what he used to say about himself, which was that he had dinked more money together with one arm than many had with two.

He was a great man with sheep, feeding tegs, one-year-old lambs, on the turnips of Bredon Hill. His fat sheep were famous when mutton was in vogue in those early days of this century. Big joints with lots of fat were produced from Cotswold or Oxford Down sheep. James Cotton was farm manager and shepherd for Mr Roberts, a man with a good eye for farming the land.

Jim Vale was Mr Roberts' carter – not an observant man. One day James Cotton was walking down Bredon Hill through the Paris Gardens on the lower slopes of the Hill. He was on his way to dinner after shepherding his flock higher up the Hill. Jim Vale was ploughing in a field known as Hempits with three horses in line driven by a plough boy. James Cotton must have been 400 yards away from the plough team but he noticed something wrong. The filler, or the horse nearest the plough, was pulling askew in an awkward fashion. James could see that the horse was pinched, or had a sore shoulder under the collar. He walked across the two fields to the carter telling him to hook the filler off and use a different animal after dinner. (The usual cure for a sore shoulder was to dress the sore place with alum and rest the animal. It is interesting that when the hair grows again on the raw place it always grows through white regardless of the colour of the horse. Years ago men used to cut a star on the front of the head of a young horse, the hair came white and the white starred horse was considered something special. A cruel practice.)

In 1911 Arthur Roberts decided to rent Old Manor Farm to Tom Archer, my father, and Harry Bailey. They had previously rented fields from Mr Roberts for pea and sprout growing. Harry Bailey and his family moved into the farm house, which had been occupied by the Wesson family. At the same time Stanley Farm was vacant because the previous tenant, Sam Eaton, had moved to Elmley Castle. So my Dad, a single man at the time, moved into Stanley Farm with Arthur Grinnel. Kate Bayliss, a quite beautiful girl from the village, daughter of Joseph Bayliss, the carpenter and wheelwright, kept house for Tom and Arthur. It is said that my mother, then Lily Westwood, soon married Dad when Kate went to the farm as his housekeeper.

Tom and Harry Bailey had a scratch team of horses to work the land. Dick with a big knee, Captain with a ridge back, Prince and Tom the nag. Ralph Pratt described the state of the land as 'as full of squitch [couch grass] as Hell is full of parsons'.

That year, 1911, Harry and Tom planted 10 acres of brussel sprouts 800 feet up on Bredon Hill. It was all a great adventure as no one had ever grown sprouts high on Cotswold-type land before. That stoney limestone had only a few inches of soil on top of hard rock. Ralph Pratt, with two horses and a double plough known as a bouting-out plough, ridged the land. The plants were set on top of the ridges.

It's one of the mysteries of farming that the soil keeps damp under the stones. Harry Bailey brought with him his own strain of sprout seed when he came to the manor from Evesham. Thus the partnership benefited from the skills of the Evesham market gardeners, as well as from the knowledge of Tom Archer's Ashton men. Together, they became specialists in their field among vegetables and fruit under Bredon Hill.

There is an old saying that 'A sheep's worst enemy is another sheep'. What it really means is that land can become sheep sick. (The land can also become sprout and cabbage sick. For example, the little area of black soil at Evesham had grown vegetables year after year for many years, and was probably vegetable sick.) The Old

Manor Farm originally farmed by the Squire and then by Arthur Roberts had always been a sheep, cattle and corn enterprise. Now, it was sheep sick. To grow vegetables there would have provided relief for that land. It was on this land therefore that, with Harry Bailey's know-how, crops of vegetables were grown par excellence. The same could not be said of Stanley Farm where the land had been neglected, and it was some years of fallow before fields like the Thurness were growing good crops.

When the First World War came in 1914 Tom and Harry had two good stables of cart horses under two carters. The horses were bought at the fairs at Gloucester and Evesham and at dispersal sales. Ralph, the carter, was pleased with his team after suffering with what could be described as 'the awkward squad' of old Dick and Captain, Prince and Tom. However, trouble arose when Percy Nind from Beckford became a buyer of horses for the Army. Yes, he bought two of Ralph's best horses in the team, and then bought a rick of clover from Stanley Farm for the Army. A gang of men came and trussed the clover, loading it at the railway station.

Although it was a trying time for carters, who did their best to hide their best horses from the Army buyers, it was important that the Army had adequate rations. A factory over the Tibblestone border at Toddington provided tinned food for the Western Front. A lot of carrots, parsnips and onions off Tom and Harry's land went to Toddington for the soldiers. Times were hard on the land when young men were called up, but the produce sold well.

When the war was over in 1919 Arthur Roberts and John Collins, Tom and Harry's landlords, decided to sell their farms. There was no security of tenure in those days. Tenants either bought the property or got out. It was obvious that Tom Archer and Harry Bailey had made some money during those eight years of tenancy but to buy 560 acres of land with farm houses, cottages, and the rest meant they had to borrow £9,000, a lot of money then.

I believe they paid off the mortgage in 1923, four years after they had borrowed it. That same year Harry Bailey became the new Lord of the Manor of Ashton under Hill.

CHAPTER THIRTEEN

THE MARKET

George Hone, the auctioneer from Tewkesbury, was a big landowner in Gloucestershire. His son, Leonard, told me that George could walk from Tewkesbury to Cheltenham without setting foot on any one else's ground. He and Fred Archer the jockey were friends who rode together on Cleeve Hill.

George Hone's auction market at Beckford opposite the inn was adequate. The poplar trees on the boundary sheltered the livestock from the weather, but the cattle stood between two rows of railings which meant that the owner or his man stood between one lot and the next. A plank of wood was suspended above the sheep and pig pens so that the auctioneer could walk from pen to pen; the floor was of blue engineering bricks. Above the pens the little brick-built office had an open window from which Mr Hone looked over the sale ring. This window had a protruding shelf where the gavel fell on the sale of each lot of cattle.

Picture the scene in the 1920s: cattle and sheep being driven from all points of the Vale and Hill every Tuesday to this village; the barking of collie dogs; the shouting of drovers. Over in the station siding cattle trucks await the animals, to transport them on the little branch railway to the homes of the buyers, either dealers or farmers. The big brass bell rings outside the office and Leonard Hone offers the first lot of sheep for sale. He stands on the plank over the sheep pens.

We read of the Raddle Man in Thomas Hardy's *The Return of the Native*; his contemporary is here at Beckford. He has come from Tewkesbury with that red mixture of iron oxide and linseed oil, ready to mark the sheep. (In fact, the Raddle Man is a frightening figure, in red overalls, with a matching face and hands. He reeks of

Raddle.) Every pen of sheep sold by Mr Hone is marked with Raddle, with the approved mark of the purchaser.

The auctioneer, dressed in Cavalry Twill breeches, cloth leggings, a Harris Tweed coat and cap, keeps up a banter with his clients, moving from pen to pen. Mr MacKie, the Scot with a club foot, follows with a limp. He is the booking clerk, calling out the pen numbers in his Highland brogue, cussing farm workers, market porters, any one in earshot. (I remember Mr MacKie, whose voice would drown the assembled crowd, as he ordered the market porters or farm workers what to do with their animals.)

Stories of Beckford Market are legion. I once heard of a farmer who sold his draft ewes, full-mouthed sheep, at Beckford, then went to Craven Arms in Shropshire for replacements. Now, there was a vogue in the twenties and thirties to colour the ewes with yellow ochre. It was supposed to make them look bigger, and I admit it was effective. The sheep at the Shropshire sale were all coloured with various hues of yellow and orange. The farmer who had sold his ewes at Beckford bought some at Craven Arms. When they arrived at the Gloucestershire farm, the shepherd immediately recognized them as the sheep sold at Beckford. 'Gaffer,' he said, 'you have bought back the ewes you sold at Beckford.'

The shepherd was right. Needless to say, the ewes settled down on the farm – home from home.

When a dealer asked in a sarcastic way the pedigree of an undersized calf for sale, Leonard's quick wit served him well. He replied,

'All I know, it was got by a porter out of a railway carriage.'

The sheep on sale at Beckford in the twenties were mainly Kerry Hill or Clun Bred, and they were served by Suffolk or Hampshire Down rams. There were a few pens of the Cotswold sheep. I kept Kerry Hills but my father saw a pen of sandy-faced Radnors at Gloucester Market and bought them for me to make up my flock. Everything was fine all the winter until the spring grass the other side of the hedge enticed the sheep through the fence. In the bottom of the old hedges the ivy grows green all the winter and the early spring. The Radnors nibbled away until the gap was big enough to break through. It seemed that every day through February, as I sat down to my tea, the phone would ring. 'Your sheep are out in Mr X's cabbages.'

But they lambed beautiful lambs that February; ten ewes had fifteen lambs, an average of one and a half each. I took them to Beckford Market. A grey-whiskered old farmer, looking at one of the ewes with what is called a craw neck, where the wool is ripped away by many battles with hawthorn hedges, said to me, 'Does that ewe get out and stray a bit?'

I said, 'I don't know much about them,' and walked away. In fact, it was perhaps the best reply.

Mr Hone said to me before the sale, 'How much do you want them to make?'

My reply was, 'They have got to go, to be sold as seen and approved.' I reckon he knew why! Good ewes and lambs were being sold at this stage.

It was pretty obvious these Radnors were wayward and they went for £2 10s a couple, a couple being a ewe and a lamb and a half. The offspring of the ones with the single lambs were soon fit for the butcher. It was a give-away price, but with the vegetable crops growing in the Vale in spring, those wandering sheep were a dangerous asset.

Mr Harry Gould, from the other side of Bredon Hill, was the purchaser of the sheep, and stories came back to me that those ewes wandered over the market garden land of that area.

Over by the little office was a coal fire where one of Mr Hone's men would hot up some glue. He was a market porter and had been getting the store cattle into some sort of order for the auction. With a steaming glue pot and a handful of numbered labels he started numbering the cattle, sticking a dab of glue on each animal's rump, then slapping the number on with his hand. The dealers had a novel way of marking the cattle they bought in Mr Hone's ring. A mysterious shape cut with a pair of scissors on the beast's rump told the dealer something. It meant nothing to me.

Harvesting at Grafton in the 1920s.

The four-horse team in the Vale near Dumbleton.

Teddy Vale, who cut corn with a bagging hook, early in the century.

Picnicking on Bredon Hill in the 1920s.

Ashton under Hill Cricket Team in the 1920s.

A study in self-sufficiency: breast ploughing the allotments, *c.* 1907.

The Squire's men sawing posts and rails with a steam engine in the 1890s.

The Star Inn, Ashton under Hill, with the Cresswell family, who were landlords before the First World War.

The Plough and Harrow Inn, Ashton under Hill. The house is now a private residence.

St Barbara's Church and moat pond, Ashton under Hill. The Revd Baker laid many to rest in the churchyard here, and his kind words of comfort are fondly remembered.

Charles Archer and his wife Lesley. Charles is the present Lord of the Manor of Ashton under Hill.

So the selling would go on, Leonard Hone encouraging and cajoling the dealers of store cattle: 'When you bid £20 for a beast, that beast is worth £25. Don't waste my time, start me at a realistic price.'

In those days professional drovers still plied their trade at the markets. They would drive cattle reasonable distances – at a price. So when the animals were sold, they went to their destination, some on foot, driven by the last of this tribe of men who had been the inbetween folk, travellers with their dogs, their sticks and strong vocal cords, while others were loaded at Beckford station, into the waiting cattle trucks supervised by Mr Johnson, that gold-braided station master.

Over the road at Beckford Inn, Fred Pope, the landlord, stood on the front steps looking like something out of a Dickens' novel. His fancy check waistcoat covered the generous belly of a man who had dined and wined well over the years. Everyone who entered the inn was greeted by this man. After Shepherd Alf Tidmarsh and Rosie his dog had driven a flock of store lambs the 2 miles from Ashton under Hill, and successfully sold them, he came with me to the inn.

'Good afternoon Master Pope. I hope you have a drop of good cider on tap.' These words from the shepherd were answered by the landlord, not in an apologetic manner but with somewhat of a curse for cider drinkers.

'We don't sell cider here today, Shepherd, only good beer.'

Alf, thirsty for the amber juice of the apple, replied sharply, 'Thank you very much. You be only interested in Whiskey drinkers.'

Together we went into the bar. I had a stone beer, ginger beer from a stone bottle. Meanwhile, the shepherd turned to me and said, 'Fred, Old Pope makes more money from his beer on Market Day, but I'll try a pint.'

As we drank old Alf Tidmarsh's eyes twinkled as he said, 'They don't know what beer is today, 'tis no stronger than cold tea. Drink another and make believe thee be drunk.'

Through the door came Little Georgie, a Grafton hawker and

small farmer. If he had sung his voice would have been counter tenor or falsetto. He saw me drinking my ginger beer and began, 'I'll tell them Chapel folks at Ashton that thee be boozing in Beckford Inn. Some of them had an open air meeting outside my place telling the world what the Lord had done for them. I be glad of a bit of lard on my bread.'

Alf and I walked together to the railings of the market where a black stallion stood, and as we walked he was telling me how Fred Pope had said to Sapper Haines as he entered the pub, 'Here's the man who won the war.' Poor Sapper never entered Beckford Inn again after that sarcastic utterance.

The stallion by the railings belonged to Bill Sexty of Bangrove, a hamlet on the outskirts of Tibblestone Hundred. Bill had been walking this big black Shire Horse he called Carburettor up and down the road past the inn for the farmers to view. It was to travel Tibblestone and beyond serving the cart mares. What a beautiful animal, over 17 hands tall with a jet black coat shining like steam coal.

Bill Sexty, who lived to be over a hundred, farmed about 100 acres and bred some fine horses. He could be described as a dog and stick farmer, who dabbled in turkeys, who had hunted twice a week in his young days. Travelling around the district he met farmers on their farms. Carburettor served some good horse flesh in the Vale and on the Hill.

Shepherd Tidmarsh said, 'I suppose, Bill, your hoss is a descendant of Bishampton Harold, that fine animal I knew when I worked over near Pershore.'

'Ay,' Bill replied. 'Carburettor is as good as he was.'

We walked away, back to the market. Alf Tidmarsh said, with a twinkle in his eye, 'I wonder whether it's true, what they say about Bill Sexty.'

I was all ears.

'Well,' the shepherd began, 'Old Bill took Carburettor to a farm on the Cotswolds. The stallion served the mare, his little fox terrier dog coupled with a bitch on the farm, and they tell me that Bill had it away with the servant girl in the tallet above the stable. The mare had a foal in due time, the bitch had pups, and the servant girl had a baby. They did the three jobs on the same day!'

When we arrived at the auction, Mr Hone had almost finished selling the cattle. What the shepherd called an outright, or an outrider, representing a firm from Oxfordshire, was selling Pettefers Mixture, a 'cure all' for ailments in sheep, and Green Oils, used to lubricate and help with difficult lambing. 'Your Dad gave me instructions to get some Pettefers Mixture and Green Oils,' said Alf.

The rep took the packets from his case, saying he would send the invoice to Archer and Bailey. These medicines were depended upon before the days of M&B and other antibiotics, and before sheep and lambs were vaccinated against dysentery and pulpy kidney disease.

Over in a little paddock next to the inn Ernie Hine had set up business as a saddler, harness-maker and cobbler. Ernie was Church Warden at the parish church, and what's referred to as 'on the door' at village dances. We opened the door to the small hut; inside the Valour Perfection stove smoked and warmed the room. Ernie's wooden hut was a meeting-place for everyone; little boys would come to watch his magical way of lining cart-horse collars with straw. (But Ralph, our carter, used to send me with a fleece of wool to reline the collars, wool being a softer material for the horses' necks than straw.)

Ernie sat at his bench mending a horse's bridle, sewing the repair with what was known as wax ends. As he worked, the thread he used was pulled through wax in his hand, making a good strong lasting thread for his needle. Ernie had so much harness around him he appeared to be sitting in the midst of leather — bridles, hip straps, cruppers, belly bands, horse collars. Ernie also repaired binder canvasses at harvest time for farmers — a master craftsman in leather, sitting there with a vice with wooden jaws holding the leather as he sewed for the farmers of Tibblestone.

As a plough boy I bought a whip off Ernie Hine. He told me that they were no longer called whips but persuaders. He also sold the lashes for whips and catapult elastic.

The cattle dealers took the trains home. Beckford Market was over until the next time. I walked up Rabbit Lane and home with the shepherd. When livestock began to be transported by cattle lorries to bigger markets it killed the little auctions and the market-place at Beckford now sports three rather good quality houses, including the new Vicarage.

Memories remain of the half-bred Hereford/Shorthorn cattle, native of Britain, and of Kerry Hill ewes of the Welsh borders. In the 1920s, when I first went to Beckford Market, cattle were red and white, the Friesians from abroad had not invaded the scene. The first herd of these black and white intruders was farmed at Gubshill Manor, near Tewkesbury.

Now the Friesians themselves are giving way to names such as Limosel, Charolais, Belgian Blue as the farming scene changes ever more. Farmers in smart suits, workers in denim now replace the breeches and leggings of the Masters and the corduroy of their men. Maybe Emmerdale and The Archers are typical of farming today. Many of the markets too, like Beckford, no longer exist. Although times must change, it seems a shame if all the old skills and the craftsmanship are to be lost.

CHAPTER FOURTEEN

HARRY BAILEY, LORD OF THE MANOR

Harry Bailey was born at Honeybourne near Evesham in the 1860s. His early introduction to the land as a young man came by way of the usual round of seasonal work on that clay. Being one of the older brothers at home he worked with hook and crook cutting wheat at harvest. He told me how on a very hot day in the field his younger brother, Jim, still at school, had been told to take Harry his mid-day dinner. But Harry worked through that day until evening without food or drink – Jim had forgotten to take his dinner to the field.

On returning home, Harry's mother was upset. She said, 'Sit at the table. I'll get you a meal.'

Harry replied, 'No. It's too late. Jim didn't bring the dinner, I'll go to bed.'

He told me how he went to bed and in his words, 'I hadn't had bit nor spot all day.'

Now that was typical of a man who was to become Lord of the Manor at Ashton under Hill. A man of steel, call it stubbornness if you like, but I call it determination.

Harry listened to Joseph Arch speaking from a farm wagon that harvest at Honeybourne, speaking for the rights of the farm labourers. But Harry Bailey was not impressed. His sights were set higher. He was going to be his own master.

The farmer at Honeybourne soon recognized Harry as a smart young man, and he was given the job as milkman, driving the pony and float to Evesham, delivering the pints and quarts to his customers.

Soon Harry married and took land at Bengeworth, growing fruit and vegetables for the market. Rubbing shoulders with some of the staid market gardeners of the day, Harry Bailey learnt the art and mystery of growing and marketing.

In those days in the late nineteenth century everything went to market in hampers made of local withy. When the fruit or vegetables were weighed, 10 lb was allowed for the weight of the hamper. Harry told me how he saw men bring back empty hampers weighing maybe 15 lb because they had been soaked in water. They then allowed 10 lb for the hamper, robbing the customer of 5 lb of produce.

What Harry Bailey was really interested in, as he took his fruit and vegetables to market with his mare Min in his dray, was good strains of seed. He perfected a sprout strain, a hard, dark green sprout which he called The Blue Variety. All this knowledge was to be valuable when he was to farm and market garden 500 acres with Tom Archer.

Harry did nothing by halves. Toothache had to be endured in those days a hundred years ago, but not with Harry. Sea Quar, an Indian quack doctor, was extracting teeth in Evesham market-place one Saturday evening. Harry was suffering and told the quack doctor to take the lot out, which he did. When he got home, Harry's wife didn't recognize her husband as he came up the path with a very swollen face. He never took to dentures, but could eat an apple perfectly with his gums.

Apart from the market garden, Harry and Tom Archer were both buying fruit on the trees in the Vale and in Oxfordshire. They both had their cobs and drays, and together they joined the Salvation Army. Harry played a sousaphone, bombardon, and Tom a euphonium. It was a recognized thing in the 1890s that men who were Salvationists prospered in business, possibly because, being teetotal, time and money were not wasted on drink.

At the turn of the century Harry had built quite a good house in Evesham, but in 1911 he and his family moved to the Old Manor Farm at Ashton under Hill as tenants to Arthur Roberts.

The war years were profitable years for Harry Bailey and Tom Archer. Then, when they bought the two farms, Harry became Lord of the Manor of Ashton under Hill in 1923. What an adventure for the farm boy from Honeybourne.

In the Tibblestone Hundred on the western slopes of Bredon Hill there was never such a deft snarer of rabbits, a better shot at fur and feather than Harry Bailey. I know because I helped him as he set snares as fast as we could walk those hills. So keen was he of the shooting and snaring on Bredon Hill that high up near the Parish Quarry he planted half an acre of parsley at the top end of the sprout field. He knew that on those bare hills the hares would be attracted to parsley and sure enough they came from all points of the compass to graze the herb.

To be fair neither Harry nor my father, Tom, were as careful as they might be with their guns. These former Little Master Men of the Market Gardens, now farming 500 acres, had never had the schooling of the big shooting syndicates. Harry, intent on protecting the crops from the ravages of pigeons and crows, would cycle along the road where the pea field stretched from the railway. His twelve-bore was cocked ready for blasting at the crows as he half-dismounted and half-fell from the bike. His gun and two dogs, Jum, an Italian greyhound, and Laddie, a fox terrier, accompanied him almost everywhere. Cartridges at 2d each from Mr Barret were bought by the hundred. A special brand of Crimson Flash was the favourite of Harry and Tom.

One very wet day on Bredon, Harry arrived home soaked to the skin after ferreting with a party of friends. His cartridges were wet from the constant rain, and without telling anyone Harry put them in the oven in the kitchen of the Old Manor. After he had changed his clothes he went out to the stable to find out how Ralph the carter had got on that wet day. Mrs Bailey was preparing tea for the family in the dining room when the cartridges started to explode. Whether it blew the door off the oven I don't remember, but Mrs Bailey did have a fright. She was used to surprises with her husband.

In later years Harry used to buy black powder cartridges cheap off Barret. They had black rings around their cream coloured cases. He provided boxes of these for me to shoot at the starlings on the strawberries. 'Keep pounding away at them, Fred boy, and get there early in the morning,' he told me.

This was classed as essential work for me, a boy of sixteen. I enjoyed those days by the quarry on Bredon where Harry and my father grew their strawberries.

Thinking back, my recollections of the Lord of the Manor are clear. Harry was a handsome man, fresh faced, with a clipped moustache, dressed for market in cord breeches, fawn leggings, and light boots which he called his tea drinkers. He wore a trilby hat with a rounded crease. In such gear Harry attended meetings of the Parish Council and School Board, of which both he and my father were members. The other members were farmers, an artist and a retired Birmingham Iron Master.

Harry was respected by one and all but the 'Top Brass' of the Parish Council, who could not understand Harry's friendship with George Palmer, an atheist and very left wing in his politics, an 'Ismael' of the tribe, never accepted by the village.

But George Palmer was useful in many ways to Harry. Obviously his left wing ideas and his outspoken views, condemning religion as an atheist, were not in agreement with Harry's ideas as a committed Christian and member of the Chapel. Saturdays in the winter months were set aside by Harry and Tom for rabbiting on the hill. George Palmer bred some useful ferrets and dogs, and was considered a member of the party.

George Palmer did a taxi service in the village with a model T Ford. Harry bought a car too, a Studebaker, but he could not drive it. George taught him to drive, and in those early days of motoring would drive the Studebaker with Harry to Gloucester or Birmingham. But Harry was not a good driver; he never got the knack of going into reverse! Impatience was one of his traits and I remember going with him to market and the car in front would not pull over. Harry Bailey passed him on the near side.

When Harry and Tom had established themselves as farmers and market gardeners they each bought a Governess Car. Tom's was light oak, which matched his chestnut cob called Polly. Harry's was dark oak and his cob was an iron grey (the name escapes me). On their journeys to Evesham shopping on Fridays, these young men cut quite a dash. Black leather, brass-mounted harness on Harry's cob, and brown-mounted harness on Polly. Polly was a dear, quiet mare, Harry's gelding was fast and difficult to catch when he grazed in Ten Furlongs. I have seen a lot of the men who worked for Harry and Tom attempting to catch that iron grey gelding. Oh yes, he tipped the two men out of that Governess Car in Port Street in Evesham one day. The mark on the mudguard stayed as a reminder until the outfit was sold.

When Harry came to Ashton under Hill he soon got involved in the Chapel. Being rather restricted as a Salvationist, he found more scope for his energy as Treasurer of the village Chapel. Harry was essentially a broad-minded man and soon he was raising money for the building of a new Chapel. Some didn't agree with draws and raffles, but Harry's ways of raising money were legion. He had friends who could be what he called tapped, and it's surprising where the money came from. The strawberry teas on the lawn of the Old Manor are memorable. I was in the market on the morning of one tea with Harry. One after another of his friends gave him baskets of cherries, currants, hampers of peas, to sell for the Chapel fund. Old Reuben Marshall from Pershore came with several baskets of fruit, another of the old Nonconformists of the Vale of Evesham.

The strawberry tea on Harry's lawn was a memorable occasion. Folk came from far and near to the Old Manor. You will gather by now that Harry Bailey did nothing by halves. The portions of strawberries given to the folk were quite generous to say the least, accompanied by lashings of cream from Tom and Harry's milking herd. The crowd that day had their nine-penny worth. Games were organized on the lawn, croquet, and a race of rabbits on strings, the rabbits, made of three-ply wood, were jogged along to the finishing line. How typical of Harry to bring rabbits into play.

Working for Harry Bailey, I gained an insight into just what made him tick. He was a fair employer but didn't suffer fools gladly. One had to do one's shot, but at the end of the day Harry always gave compliments on a good job done.

Hoeing crops had to be done meticulously. If Frank and I were hoeing mangolds at the end of the day and, like other hobbledehoys, straightening our backs a little, the cry would come from Mr Bailey as he entered the field, 'Bend your backs.' He and my father learnt their farming the hard way and jobs were required to be done properly, and not what was known as shuffled.

After early morning strawberry picking the men were given orders for hoeing the sprouts after breakfast. Harry had noticed that Walter, not one of the best men in the field but useful for repairing implements, general bricklaying and odd jobs, had been hoeing the previous day with me and two more hobbledehoys. Harry came from the wash-house at the back of the Old Manor after he had his breakfast carrying a new hoe. 'Walter,' he called across the yard, 'here's a hoe that will keep up with the men not the boys.'

Walter made some excuse, but the point was that Harry then brought his hoe from the wash-house and walked alongside Walter to the sprout field. He hoed all day beside Walter. Good company, but he was like that.

Whether I got preferential treatment from Harry when I worked on the farm I don't know. He did give me some interesting jobs, snaring and trapping, ferreting and shooting. I do believe that he treated me as a son, for he had two daughters and lost his only son in his teens. I remember his saying to Dad one day, 'You know, I reckon Fred aught to become a Parson. He doesn't care whether the cow calves or the bull breaks his neck.'

On Evesham market day, either Dad or Harry met us at the market, sometimes they both came. Dad used to give me a shilling to get a cup of cocoa and some lardy cakes from Churchleys little café in the alley. That was fine, but Harry was generous and once gave me half a crown; I thought that I would never want money ever again!

My two bosses were different as chalk and cheese, yet they complemented each other. Harry was a very shrewd market gardener and fruit grower. He recognized the fact that crops like sprouts and peas needed what he called a little help (some fertilizer). He wasn't so good with the cattle and sheep – that's where Dad excelled. They both bought week-old calves at local markets. Harry, not a patient man, didn't reckon to spend all day until the ideal animal was in the ring. If the cowman wanted two calves, two calves he bought. Dad, on the other hand, would spend hours judging the cross-bred Hereford calves and placing four fingers between their shoulder blades, the proof that the calf would turn into a good beef animal.

I remember so well several nights with Harry on Bredon Hill, catching rabbits with the long net. He took me, Frank, Geoff, and my brother Tom, and showed us the art and mystery of using the long net. This Lord of the Manor was a great sportsman and good to us boys. Amusing incidents come to mind. On wet days Harry was intent on getting his men working, but they were intent on sheltering in the hovel. The hovel had a corrugated iron roof which made the rain sound heavier.

'It's a bit lighter George, the rain is clearing,' Harry would say.

George would reply, 'There's a few too many spots on one, and it still looks black over Bill's Mother's.'

Harry, with a sack over his shoulders and persuasive as ever, would eventually entice his men from the hovel.

In 1927 Harry bought a very nice Hillman saloon car, about the best car in the village. He took me up on the Cotswolds one day to look at a field of peas he was buying. Harry thought it a bit of a come-down to change gear up hills and we chugged up Broadway Hill in top gear. I'll never forget the farmer's reaction when we knocked at his door. He had been having an after-dinner nap and was rubbing his half-closed eyes. Confronted by Harry Bailey, he had a shock when, after a few words introducing ourselves, Harry looked him straight in the face asking, 'What's the name of the child?'

The farmer was nonplussed, and he had to be told that the expression was an Evesham one for 'How much?'

Harry bought the peas, but walking through the crop hares were popping up everywhere in the pea rows. From what I gathered that day Harry would have forgotten the peas if only he could have spent a day shooting hares.

The peas on that Cotswold farm were picked by men who are widely known as 'The Gentlemen of the Road'. My brother took a lorry load of these travellers up there from our farm, where the pea harvest had ended. They erected their bivouacs under a wall, where a row of beech trees gave some shelter.

It was my job to weigh the peas and dole out the pea checks with the legend H.B. on each metal disc, Harry Bailey's mark. When my brother loaded the lorry each evening with the day's picking, he exchanged checks for cash for any of the travellers who needed it. Most of the men waited until Friday.

I learnt a lot from this unusual Lord of the Manor. First of all, on leaving school, as what Dad called a strapper to Harry Bailey, I learnt how to snare rabbits, to handle ferrets, to paunch and hock rabbits. Later, in the field lessons in market gardening, I was taught the way to use a setting pin and plant sprouts, beans, and so on, and skills such as the proper way to hoe. Most important, Harry taught me how to set a ladder in a fruit tree, to keep it fairly upright and to place the top in a fork of the tree. We learnt how to pick strawberries the proper way, pinching the stalk with thumb and fingernail. These are just a few of the lessons learned from Harry Bailey.

Later in the autumn of 1927, the partners decided to buy another bull. Samson was old and heavy, and a young bull was required to serve the young heifers. A sale at Gloucester included some bulls from Mr Stephens of Netherton, near Elmley Castle. It was decided to attend that sale on the Saturday and I was invited to accompany Dad and Harry. That morning Harry was not well, having a stomach upset. We met at the Old Manor and he couldn't decide whether to go to the bull sale. In the end he did come, Dad driving, with Harry and me riding in the back.

They bought a very nice young bull for forty guineas and then we went to the Wessex Hotel for dinner. There was always the same menu at this eating-house in Kings Square. The waitress came and said her piece: 'Roast beef, roast pork, boiled mutton. Apple tart, plum tart, rice pudding.'

One big difference between Dad and his partner was that Harry had a wonderful digestion and could eat most things, while Dad was a martyr to indigestion. (If any tea was left in the pot at teatime at the Old Manor, Harry would always clear it up.) Both Dad and I decided on roast beef, Harry ordered the pork, which Dad thought a bit risky with a stomach upset. The meal finished, Harry was soon fast asleep. He used to tell me that he could fall asleep before I could count to a hundred, another difference between the partners, Dad was a light sleeper. On one visit to Wales, buying sheep, the partners stayed at a hotel where a clock struck every quarter of an hour outside the bedroom window. Harry slept solidly but Dad was awake all night.

After dinner that Saturday at Gloucester we three, Harry Bailey, Dad and myself, led the bull from the market to the station, and put him in a pen ready for the railway men to load him into a cattle truck to travel to Beckford Station. Tom Whittle and I walked to Beckford to meet the 8.20 train that night, and led the bull 2 miles to Ashton under Hill. It was a moonlit night I remember, we met few cars, and the bull was put in a pen at the Old Manor.

On 13 October that year Harry Bailey died and a great character was missed in the village. Ralph the carter with Flower pulling the dray followed the hearse up the village to the Chapel. The whole bed of the dray was covered with flowers.

CHAPTER FIFTEEN

STANLEY FARM, THE BAILIFF'S HOUSE

Being born at Stanley Farm and living there through my school-days and early life on the farm, I inherited a wealth of folklore and tales of earlier occupants of the house. Later, from 1940 to 1970, I farmed 150 acres of Stanley Farm.

Jim Stanley, a respected Church Warden, lived there and farmed the land in the middle of the 1800s and his name is remembered. Squire Baldwyn employed bailiffs there. One came from Somerset, and it proved difficult for the local farmworkers to understand his dialect. Terms like 'thick mow' meant a hay rick.

After this occupant the house remained empty and was said to be haunted. Was it rats? As I lay awake on winter nights, they circled the hollow wall of the timber-framed building making a noise like thunder. They took the soap from the back kitchen and seemed to prefer Lifebuoy.

Charles Slatter, a Cotswold man, farmed well, kept a good herd of cows, looked after his men at haymaking and harvest. Charles farmed Stanley Farm at the time of the reorganization of the Squire's Estates, and was a good employer of labour. A pretty able horseman was Charles, who hunted with the Croome Hunt. On a window-pane in the breakfast room at the farm I often admired Charles' signature, cut with a diamond on the glass. Jim Barnet, who worked for Slatter, killed pork pigs and lambs for his men. Horse radish grew profusely in the garden of Stanley Farm, planted by Jim Barnet. I fought a losing battle with this persistent plant in the 1950s. Jim told me of the wonderful crop of celery he grew for Charles Slatter. He said he filled the trench with soccage from the cow shed – what a descriptive word!

Sam Eaton followed. He was a keen hunting man who seemed to live astride a horse and walked the foxhound puppies, known as a puppy-walking, for the Croome Hunt. I gather this was at his own expense but the puppies went to a show in the autumn and prizes were given to the best young hound. Sam Eaton's wife had reared turkeys in the Stanley Farm rick yard and kept poultry, both laying hens and for the table. She sold her produce in the local market at Tewkesbury and she, more than her husband, earned their living. Sam was a dog and stick farmer, and, on leaving the farm, left the fields full of weeds.

Tom Archer, my father, came to Stanley Farm in 1911 when his partner came to the Old Manor. As a boy, I explored this rambling house, trying to discover its secrets. The prayer room at the top of the stairs spoke of the age-old battle between Catholics and Protestants, when the Government and the King treated the folk with opposite beliefs very badly. I imagined the worship of God going on in secret in that room behind closed doors. Was that the reason for one of the stairs being six inches higher than the rest? Folk told me that if an intruder broke in at night that stair would trip them up, a clever hazard.

When schoolboy friends came from the nearby town, a town where the streets were lit by electricity and there was indoor sanitation, Stanley Farm, lit by paraffin and candles with its privy up the garden, was like an Aladdin's Cave. What a place for hide and seek and cricket in the rickyard and paper chases on the hill!

On leaving school it was plough driving for me, with Carter Pratt. It was the hardest work I remember on that Gloucestershire clay, when the days dragged on, but how peaceful sleep came at night after a while spent listening to the wireless and dipping into the *Cheltenham Echo*.

Those first winters on Stanley Farm were bitter. My job at that time was under cowman to Tom Whittle. What a mine of information he was. He had broken in horses, built ricks like cottages, and thatched them too, and had an eye for farming things.

Walking the hedgerows with him once, he suddenly said, 'There's a scythe sned, a scythe handle.' Sure enough, there in a tree was a twisted branch the perfect shape for a handle. Old Jack Hunting did the rest, fitting it to Tom's scythe.

Jack Hunting was one of the farm workers. Working in the fields with these men who had little formal education, it was apparent to me that they possessed many skills of their own. It was 'Do It Yourself', 1920s style. Jack was no exception. If the shaft broke on a horse rake or wagon, old Jack, with his primitive tools and a lot of know-how, replaced them with pieces of ash cut from the coppice. He repaired ladders, made rough gates known as heavers, and spreaders for the plough harness; he was a wizard of a rough carpenter.

Tom Whittle was also a cow doctor of no mean repute, and had an eye for an ailing beast. We dosed the scouring calves, we treated ringworm and husk on the yearlings. Tom knew a thing or two about the animals.

The cows used for rearing calves were getting old and so Dad bought twelve red Shorthorn heifers from Ireland. They were a picture. Our bull was a bit too heavy to serve them, so they were sent to a neighbour's farm. As the heifers grazed the Kersoe Grounds, Tom and I had foddered the store cattle on the hill and came to feed the heifers in the field. One was missing, and we found a dead calf the size of a hare, lying under the hedge. Tom knew immediately, and said to me, 'Contagious abortion.'

'Oh,' I said, 'but cows do slip their calves sometimes.'

Tom replied, 'This ain't a slip, the heifer has cast her calf.' It was serious. All twelve cast their calves at about six months.

After these heifers had aborted, they gave about a gallon of milk each per day. Away from the other milk cows, I looked after six of these heifers above the little hamlet of Paris on Bredon Hill. It was here in an old barn the heifers suckled a calf each. No one mentioned Brucellosis, and luckily the disease didn't affect me.

Ploughing on Stanley Farm with the four-horse team is a nostalgic memory in more ways than one. Those long mornings from 7 until

3 o'clock dinner, trudging on the clay, clinging to the clay. There was a quietness about the field, with just the jingle of harness, the squeak of the plough wheels.

A typical day with the four-horse team at plough comes back vividly to me. I met Ralph the carter at the stable in the half light of the wintery morning at just after 7 o'clock. He had been feeding the horses since 6 o'clock. We made our way to The Thurness, a 20-acre field half a mile away. I was astride the foremost horse, Ralph walking behind carrying a paddle, a little spade used to scrape the trash from the plough. Under the hedge we had out bait at 10 o'clock. Ralph had bread and cheese and cold tea. I had bread and lard flavoured with rosemary, and cold tea.

At 3 o'clock we took the Groaten Road home. Groaten is a Roman road where lots of coins were found. The horses took their turn to drink at the trough. As they bent their necks their collars slipped and each one threw his collar back as they straightened. Ralph put their bait, or chaff, oats and roots, in the manger and the four horses took their places as we took their harness off their backs, known as ungearing them. Ralph climbed the tallet ladder to the loft above and filled their racks with clover. We went to our dinner.

When we came back to the stable Ralph was busy cutting clover from the nearby rick and carrying it up to the tallet. I cleaned out the stable.

At 5 o'clock by the light of a lantern slung on a plough trace we sat on the bench in the Gras house for a while before turning out the team to the field called The Close, and making our own way home.

One thing which is true of life for a boy on the land was the diversity of jobs to do. Some were interesting, some what we called sading. No, boring was never mentioned! These jobs were given to boys and hobbledehoys as a sort of rough education. On Stanley Farm, we were not allowed to think that work was easy. So we were sent pulling charlock among the peas, runner beans, kidney beans, and who carried the chaff, the dustiest job at threshing? The boys, of course.

So life on the farm was learnt a little at a time, a life of animals and folk. Oh, I knocked a few gateposts down with the wheel of a muck cart, I broke Harry Bailey's whet stone when we were reaping, when I was tying sheaves, and I lost his best ferret when I was rabbiting. It's all part of the growing-up process, and all part of life on the land.

CHAPTER SIXTEEN

TWENTIETH-CENTURY FARMERS

BECKFORD

While Mr Collins and Mr Roberts, followed by Mr Bailey, were Lords of the Manor at Ashton under Hill, Captain Case occupied that position at Beckford. He was a man who delegated much of the responsibility of his office to Jimmy Partinton, his bailiff.

Jimmy farmed the land as if it was his own. He grew heavy crops of cereals, fertilized by the manure from his dairy herd, but Jimmy was essentially a sheep man. He was his own shepherd on Bredon Hill, where he rode his hunter attending to the flock daily. In the early days, in the 1920s, Jimmy ran a flock of pedigree Oxford Down sheep but soon found that his breed produced joints too big for the modern housewife.

On the death of Captain Case, Beckford Hall was left to the Roman Catholic Church and became what is known as a Salesian Novitiate, where students are trained for the mission field.

At Beckford Manor, which was a manor only by name, Captain Freeman farmed a little estate; it was a pleasure farm for this retired Army officer, who reared pheasants on Doe Banks and held shooting parties in season. Of his impact on the village and the Hundred I have no record. He was followed by another captain, one Captain Davey. He and his wife are well remembered in Beckford for their generosity and care of the village people. Mrs Davey, an Italian lady, did many good works for the Nursing Association, and the school; she also excelled at helping the working folk of the village in the early thirties during the national slump. The couple were good employers with two gardeners; the estate was kept spick and span, and the local institutions were always welcome to hold fêtes and flower shows.

We are always conscious of the clay land of Tibblestone but a vein of sand stretched alongside Carrants Brook. The sand was near the surface at Wilson Bedenham's little farm. Wilson, a product of Evesham, was a cunning market gardener. He grew strawberries and vegetable crops, but he made his name with asparagus crowns, or roots. The one- or two-year-old roots were easily forked out of this sandy soil and bought by the clay land gardeners who grew the finest asparagus.

Mr Bedenham also opened a sand pit, where local folk could buy sand by the cart load in those days before mechanization. I know, because I knocked down one of his gateposts as I came through with a cart load of sand from his pit. The repercussions of this incident got me in trouble because it was reported to my father and Harry Bailey. I remember Mr Bedenham as rather a strange man. When Tom Archer and Harry Bailey attended farm sales, Wilson would be there too and if they were interested in either horses or implements you could be sure that whatever they had their eye on, then so did Wilson. When they bought Blackbird, a handy little cart-horse, Wilson moaned, 'Ah, I wanted that blessed little black un.'

Mind you, Tom and Harry had both been in the Salvation Army Band with Wilson and one of the officers described him as 'All God Almighty and tears'. However, his testimony was not one to inspire, as he declared from the market-place, 'Before I was converted I hadn't got a rag to my back nor shoes to my feet. Now I've got a donkey and cart and a bicycle, all paid for. My wife's my own and my kids are my own.'

It's also said that at one meeting he came out with a very odd philosophy: 'If you don't repent you will be working for the Devil with a wooden pick and shovel, digging taters by the bushel on the turnpike road, and what about if you woke up one morning and found yourself dead in the bottom of the bottomless pit of Hell. Where would you be then?'

It seems a shallow sort of religious experience that Wilson Bedenham had.

On the Grafton boundary of Beckford, Messrs Woodward created a prolific fruit farm and built two large greenhouses early in the twentieth century. They were a forward-looking enterprise at a time when cultivation under glass was in its infancy. So large were these greenhouses, I believe that the land under glass was cultivated with horses in between the crops of lettuce and tomatoes. The open land grew crops of fruit, and Messrs Woodward opened a sand pit in Rabbit Lane, employing men to work there and to drive their lorries.

GRAFTON

Another manor farm by name only is the home of the Crump family. John Crump, who farmed at Grafton at the turn of the century, was a successful farmer. He employed students of agriculture before the First World War, and taught them the basics of farming the land.

John Crump was followed by his son, Harry, a very good judge of cattle, who bred, reared and fattened some fine Shorthorn cross Hereford bullocks. Here was a man who gave me lots of good advice, and a man with a dry sense of humour. He advised me to buy some bullocks in Tewkesbury Market one April; they looked poor but they pitchpoled in price by November. We borrowed his seed barrow every year to plant clover and grass seeds. It went all over Tibblestone. Harry worked hard in the old-fashioned way, but always found time to go to the cinema on market days in Tewkesbury.

Some of his wit I recall. Talking of a neighbour who died, Harry said to me, 'He was a careful man you know, Fred. He would make a bottle of beer last two days.'

Like all farmers in those days Harry was dubious of new methods and I remember him asking me at market, 'Do you have your cows served by artificial insemination?'

To which I replied, 'Yes.'

He thought a minute and then said, 'I had mine done yesterday, but I don't think she enjoyed it very much.'

It was always Large White Pigs crossed with a Large Black for Mr Crump. They produced what is known as sheeted piglets, much favoured for fattening.

Since Harry's death some years ago the farm has been worked by his two sons. Yes, they have a tractor and bale their hay, but they farm in much the same way as their father and grandfather farmed before them. It's a joy to drive past Manor Farm, Grafton, where the crops are grown in rotation, and calves are reared on suckler cows. Henry and Peter keep up a tradition, caring for the land. They will never make a fortune but there is a great degree of conservation, a farm where the land is not purged with nitrogen.

HINTON ON THE GREEN

At the northern end of the Tibblestone Hundred is the village of Hinton on the Green. Only about 2½ miles from the town of Evesham this village retained a very rural image until the last few years.

The land is some of the strongest clay land on the Worcestershire/Gloucestershire borders. The village remained in Gloucestershire until the boundary changes of 1931. The River Isbourne, reputed to be the only river in England which runs north for the whole of its length, produced the power to run a water mill for grinding corn.

While villages like Ashton under Hill, Grafton and Beckford nestle under Bredon's 1,000 ft off-shoot of the Cotswolds, Hinton sits among the market gardens and farms in the Vale a little farther from the hill.

The two main farms at Hinton are the Manor Farm and Ballards Farm. Jimmy Marshall, a legendary market gardener at the turn of the century, occupied Ballards Farm. One hears stories of great crops of cabbages and peas, with eight peas in a pod, in those early days. When Squire Baldwyn sacked Judy Vale, one of his carters, Judy came to work for Jimmy Marshall and my uncle drove plough for him. Judy was a bit of what Uncle called 'on the sawney side', and he let Uncle Jim hold the plough tails and Judy drove the four-horse team. 'What will the Master say if he sees us?' was his constant fear. Hinton had a railway station on the old Midland Railway to Birmingham and that's where Jimmy Marshall's product was sent.

Mr Llewellen farmed Downrip Farm and the number of smallholders in Hinton was considerable. They knew their land and grew their strawberries, sprouts and asparagus.

Mr John Eaton followed Jimmy Marshall at Ballards Farm. He produced beef and lamb in those difficult times between the wars. He bred his own Hereford bulls and sold some useful animals. John Eaton was a level-headed farmer, who served on the District Council with my father. Both as blue Conservatives as was possible. His carter, Charlie Freeman, was a great character who could sing and recite at concerts.

Frank Sheaf farmed the Manor Farm and at that time the house was cold in winter. A friend of mine visited him many years ago. The fire was burning brightly in the sitting-room, a log fire, but what a log! Mr Sheaf had put a whole tree trunk into the fireplace with the other end balanced on a chair in the middle of the room. It saved him sawing up the logs; as the trunk burned he simply moved the chair closer in.

I don't think Frank Sheaf dabbled in market gardening in those years between the wars, when so many farmers in desperation turned from corn growing to cash crops of vegetables and fruit. In those days when the horse ruled, it was quite common for six horses to be hitched to a single-furrow plough to cultivate clay land. Parts of Greville Hall Farm north of the village grew hawthorn bushes and trees forming scrub land impossible to walk through. The local hunt found it difficult to flush the foxes from such places. Clay land does grow hawthorn and did grow great elm trees, while on the limestone Cotswold-type hill of Bredon beeches flourish.

Politics must be considered when we look at Hinton on the Green, for before 1931 Hinton was in the Cirencester and Tewkesbury Constituency. At elections in the twenties Hinton had no polling booth, and the ones in the village who had a vote were obliged to travel to Ashton under Hill. There were few cars in Ashton or Hinton, but Dad and his partner, Mr Harry Bailey, taxied the potential Tories from Hinton to Ashton under Hill to vote. How did they know who to pick up and take to the polling station? Mr

John Eaton, Mr William Newman and Mr Frank Sheaf, all dyed in the wool Tories, told them who to take to Ashton.

In between the wars, when asparagus was King in the Vale of Evesham, Mr William Newman grew excellent asparagus at Hinton on the Green. As a member of the Asparagus Growers Association, which was based in Badsey, he was a successful competitor at the Asparagus Show, winning prizes. Mr Newman was a progressive market gardener who had a farm shop on the main road selling his produce, particularly plums from his plantation. I recall him selling Pershore Plums at 1s for 14 lb in the 1930s.

In those days the market gardeners of the Vale grew Royal Sovereign strawberries and varieties such as Sir Joseph Paxton and Bedfords. Mr Newman sold Dad some plants of a new variety known as Huxleys Giant or Evesham Unknown. Massive crops of these vigorous plants took over strawberry growing in the early thirties.

Before the war New House Farm, Hinton on the Green, was a poor farm, the pastures were covered with creeping bramble bushes. The War Agricultural Committee took over this holding and with Fordson tractors and ploughs, driven by Land Girls, the farm was completely transformed. They fertilized the land and grew good crops of wheat. Over at Greville Hall and the boundary of Tibblestone the farmer was cultivating about half the land, the remainder was hawthorn scrub. The WAR AG cleared it with bulldozers, ploughed it and planted rye followed by wheat.

After the war Mr Joe Newman, William's son, took over New House Farm and the Manor Farm at Hinton on the Green. He brought with him a new meaning for agriculture, a skill in taming clay land. A caterpillar tractor and plough exposed land 9 inches deep, which had never before seen the light of day. It's true the four-horse team had skimmed the top 5 inches, but Joe's tractor and his knowledge of the land yielded good crops of field beans, wheat, and such like, keeping to some form of rotation.

Frozen peas had arrived in the shops by this time, and here at Hinton acres of peas were grown for what is known as vineing, with a modern method of threshing the pods. I remember Joe's pick-up baler when the straw from his combine was tied up in swiss rolls weighing 28 lb, a far cry from the massive bales of today.

Joe Newman had a feel for the land, but this man also made time for activities in the village. Tennis on the Manor lawn, bell-ringing in the church tower, and rough shooting with neighbours over his land. For some years he served on the Rural District Council, a useful member who knew every footpath and ditch in the village.

CHAPTER SEVENTEEN

THE GREAT OUTDOORS

WILDLIFE ON THE HILL

The Tibblestone, Bredon Hill in particular, was a grassy country. Although the inclosures of the eighteenth century did give a semblance of order to the Hundred which before was more Common Land, the country folk did consider the grassland to be their playground. No one insisted on footpaths being cleared, men went to work in the fields taking the shortest cut. There was a code of conduct and dogs were strictly under control. Since the railways and the motor car and the infiltration from the towns battles go on for rights of way, something which was unnecessary years ago.

In the Tibblestone Hundred the fox hounds often met at the marker stone at Teddington Hands. It is on the edge of the Hundred, but years ago when the Hundred took in more villages this stone was more central.

The hill of Bredon was hard going for the hunt, a strain on horse and hound to rise from the sea level of the Vale to 1,000 feet, then perhaps do this a second time. The harriers fared better, hunting hare which provided better sport as hares keep to their territory, just a few fields is their limit. The farmers who hunted with the harriers rode cobs, were dressed in breeches and gaiters, and sported bowler hats. This was certainly not a stockbroker affair with ladies looking as if they'd come straight from the hairdressing salon.

We hear so much today about wildlife as if it had just been discovered. But this is not so! Working with old Jack Hunting and Shepherd Tidmarsh taught me more about the ways of animals and birds than any text book. A rare bird arrives today and the twitchers pursue it in their hundreds with their cameras with strong lenses. I wonder, does it do anything for conservation? Rabbits are back after myxomatosis. They always made a good meal for the farm worker and his family. Jack would tell me how to pick a good young rabbit for the pot, something gained by experience, and that buck rabbits tasted strong in the breeding season and milky does don't make good eating. He never told me why it is good policy to paunch a rabbit when it is still warm. The flesh will go green if they are not gutted the same day. A hare is never paunched until it has been hung for a while.

There has been a big reduction in the sky lark population, probably a million birds have been lost. This is said to be because of loss of habitat – how I hate that word (there is a shop of that name in a town near the Tibblestone). As chemicals clean up so-called weeds, the land is never rested, larks have so few places to nest. During the winter of 1931 hordes of skylarks attacked the spring cabbages in a field called Hempits. Similar to wood pigeons, they fed on the young cabbage plants. The flocks of larks moved from one end of the field to the other. It was my job with a 410 gun to shoot at them. The birds would have ruined the crop otherwise.

Dad said when he had shot a number of birds, 'We will have a lark pie.'

That evening, under the light of the oil lamp, with my brother, we picked the feathers from the larks. The pie was tasty the following day. It was a one-off affair. It seemed a pity looking back that the lark, a lovely songster, had to pay the penalty for the loss of the cabbages.

Up on the Hill the harriers circled the stone-walled fields chasing the hares which seemed to be numerous. I used to walk the field by the stone quarry with my gun, but the last hare I shot cried like a child. I swore that never again would I shoot at those beautiful creatures.

HARE AND HOUNDS

Charlie Heath, ex-Birchfield Harriers, was a sort of sports fanatic, keeping fit in those early days of the century, the trainer of the football team. He organized paper chases all over Tibblestone, called Hare and Hounds. These began at the village cross at Ashton under Hill, and often stretched the whole length of Tibblestone, ending at that famous landmark at Teddington Hands, the Tibblestone itself. These paper chases were always held on Saturdays. Charlie arrived at the village cross at 9 o'clock. He had with him a linen satchel full of scraps of paper he had torn up the previous evening. (Today when litter is a newsworthy topic, one may frown at bits of paper being scattered over the countryside. But paper, as opposed to plastic, disappears after the first storm of rain.)

Choosing the Hare, the boy to be followed, was left to this ex-Birchfield Harriers member, who at fifty years of age still thought nothing of a 7 or 8 mile run. On several occasions, the Hare, I remember, was Jonathan, a fourteen-year-old who played football and cricket for his school.

'Now Lads,' Charlie spoke sharply to us in his broad Birmingham accent, 'give Jonathan about five minutes before you chase after him, and he will keep off standing crops and you must do the same.'

The art of the Hare is to make false tracks, lead the Hounds astray, and to be sparing with the paper. Jonathan led the Hounds up to Bredon Summit, coming down to Grafton Firs where the badger earths go deep into the limestone. Then he made a false track with the paper pieces towards Benedicts Pool above Beckford, climbing the hill by the quarry, coming down, outside Tibblestone, to Pig Lane in Worcestershire. From here he took the track to Tibblestone, down Crashmore Lane, crossing the boundary at Carrants Brook. The Hounds were way behind and Jonathan rested at the Tibblestone. When the pack arrived at the landmark Charlie, who had followed their semi-circular run with field-glasses from the road, took the party to Teddington Hands Inn treating them to ginger beer and crisps.

Jonathan did several stints as the Hare across Tibblestone, but was never caught.

BIRD BATTING AND SPARROW SHOOTS

In the last years of the nineteenth century, when poverty in the villages was real and meat was a luxury, poachers with long nets caught rabbits on Bredon Hill. Some landowners ignored the poachers, but pheasants and partridges were sacrosanct. Other villagers on dark winter nights prowled the hawthorn hedges of Tibblestone with nets on poles. They took part in what was known as bird batting. Two poles with a net between caught the roosting birds from the hedges. One man held a lantern, another hit the hedge on the opposite side with a heavy stick, and as the birds went towards the light of the lantern they were caught in the net. Many a good meal has been had by the family from bird batting.

Sparrow shoots no doubt were a forerunner of present-day clay pigeon shoots. Sparrows for these events, which took place in a field behind the White Hart Inn at Ashton under Hill, and in a field behind Teddington Hands Inn, and opposite the Beckford Inn, were caught by bird batting. The house sparrow roosts under the thatch of barns and in rick yards.

Ralph Davies, a countryman well known to me, with his brother Jack, caught the sparrows for the shoots. Guns lined up and bets were taken – 2 to 1 on the bird, or 2 to 1 on the gun – and the sparrows were released from their cages. My old friend Ralph told me that the guns were charged with what he called dust shot, small-sized ammunition. However primitive the sport appears today, or cruel, just think of the corn-fed pheasants, half-tame, driven by the beaters over the guns as the syndicate shoots its annual battue from October to February.

Villagers of Tibblestone were involved in the sparrow shoots as out scouts. They were posted on the edge of the field to shoot the birds that escaped the members of the shoots. These out scouts, Ralph said, made a picture with their muzzle-loader guns and black powder giving off clouds of dark smoke when they fired. The whole affair was geared to gambling. Who held the betting money, and who paid? The truth is lost in history.

TWO SORTS OF CRICKET

It seems to me that professionalism has crept into the leisure side of village life where so much emphasis is placed on being the winning side and looking the part. This does apply to cricket in the first instance. Now men turn up on Saturdays and Sundays immaculately dressed in creased flannels. They arrive in their Range Rovers, their BMWs, a far cry from yesterday's transport. The pitch has been manicured, every scrap of grass mown to extinction on the outfield. Cow pats? No cow has grazed this sacred few acres for years. The new villagers will not permit such infringement on their cream flannels. In the pavilion the figures of batting averages, of bowling figures, are studied. Cricket teams compete in league games. The dropped catch, the miss field, oh, that could cost the game. It is a game; that must never be forgotten. It's also good to win, but I recall that great captain of our team in Tibblestone, a colonel in the Army, who said these words at the Monday Selection Committee Meeting, 'I realize we shall be short of our best fast bowler on Saturday. Some of you want to cancel the match. For me the game is paramount, whether we win or lose.'

The young village cricketers of yesterday had their schooling in some farm rick yard where the stumps were rick pegs of withy and the hay rick acted as wicket keeper. Until darkness fell on summer evenings I bowled and batted against other boys of my age. Maybe it was a good schooling, so different from net practice in the corner of the cricket field.

Arthur Thomson, a dog and gun farmer who lived in a wood on the slopes of Bredon Hill, apparently was a useful bowler. W.G. Grace came to this Tibblestone village playing in a charity match. One of Arthur's inswingers bowled out the great man. Charlie Moore, ladder- and hurdle-maker and cricket umpire, was anxious for the crowd to see a good match. A bit late, Charlie shouted, 'No ball.'

Arthur looked at this umpire, saying, 'I bowled him middle stump.'

'Ah, but,' Charlie replied, 'folks un't come to see thee bowl, they be come to see Grace bat.'

We must not forget that villages have become more middle class, class conscious, which is not altogether a good thing. The village blacksmith of the twenties, dressed in grey flannels with belt and braces, middled the bowling pretty well. To see Archie at full stretch, those arms like legs of mutton, tattooed and bronzed, hit six after six was a delight.

All the team were not like Archie Butler with his haymaker strokes, a man who had replied to an advert in the local paper: 'WANTED a Blacksmith, preferably one who can play cricket.' C.K. the captain, a farmer and comedian, employed Archie for years as Blacksmith.

Ewart Morrison played a lot of cricket in the villages of the Tibblestone Hundred. He was an unassuming area manager for the National Farmers' Union Assurance. A public school man who mixed so well with the cider-soaking farm men of the Vale villages. It soon became apparent that Ewart was more than a village cricketer, he had county qualities. He played a couple of years for Gloucestershire – a bowler who put the fear of God into both county and village players, a useful bat, and one of the best slip fielders who ever played for his county.

One Saturday without a fixture for Gloucestershire, Ashton, the Tibblestone village where Ewart lived high on Bredon Hill, were so pleased to have him on their team. In his smart flannels, his county cap, Ewart came in first wicket down for the village team. That's the least Captain C.K. could do for his brother-in-law. The visiting bowler was putting the ball wide but not wide enough for Charlie, the umpire, to call a wide. One ball Ewart padded away towards the square leg boundary. The bowler's 'How's that?' got Charlie's finger giving the dread signal 'Out. LBW'. Ewart was too much of a gentleman to argue with Umpire Charlie, but our cowman said that he used a word as he went up the pavilion steps 'As unt in the Bible or the Prayer Book'.

Old-time cricket fascinated me. Umpires were sometimes like a twelfth man in the team. One 'How's that?' to Charlie got the reply 'Not out but if it occurs again it will be'. Part of Dumbleton is in

Tibblestone, and they produced some fine cricketers. One chap made 100 against Ashton, but then played the ball with bat and pad. Charlie said 'Out'. Our Captain's retort was 'He played the ball with bat and pad, he can't be out'.

Charlie, not to be ruled over, replied, 'The ball hit him on the leg, and any road I wants my tea.'

Men like Charlie and Archie are no longer walking the hallowed turf. Charlie once hit a ball which ended up in Gloucester twenty miles away – it dropped in a railway wagon! The likes of him are not often seen on Saturday afternoons. A straight bat is the mode today. Wild strokes are risky, one could get caught on the boundary. After all it's not only one's batting averages that are at stake, but also the honour of the village.

CHAPTER EIGHTEEN

SELF-SUFFICIENCY IN
THE FIELD AND HOME

A typical farm labourer of Tibblestone after the turn of the century would buy himself a pair of boots with his harvest money, waterproofs to keep his feet dry during the winter. These, with leather leggings or putties, were a must in the fields of the Hundred.

But what of this man's cottage economy, his allotment or big garden? The privy up the garden had a pit behind the two-seater. On a moonlight night the man of the house emptied this pit, a cesspit covered with a stone slab. A bucket of soil with its little shovel provided a covering when the family had their daily movement. This, with a sprinkle of disinfectant powder, kept the little house free of smells. Emptying the privy was not the unpleasant job one would imagine. The bacteria from the effect of the soil had turned the contents of the pit into a compost. Wheeled to the garden or allotment in the countryman's barrow, our friend had fertilizer for his crops. Rhubarb shoulder high, potatoes, beans, peas, and so on. For his celery, the trench was filled with his compost and cow parsley from the roadside verge. The country cottager made use of things around him. Nothing was wasted.

Provisions bought with the 30s a week wage were supplemented by food from the allotment, the fowl house, the pig sty. It was usual for the cottager to buy, for a week's wages, a hog pig, a castrated young boar. If a gilt, or young sow, was put in the sty for fattening it was never killed when in season because the bacon was said to not take the salt. Some put the sow to the young boar some weeks before it was killed to ensure that it was not, as the locals said, 'on brimming'. What thought went into the rearing and fattening of an animal which provided meat and bacon for the year.

Pig clubs were formed in the Tibblestone villages where the members paid a few pence a week to insure the pig against disease or death. When food was rationed members of pig clubs could get balancer meal in place of their bacon coupons. This meal was supposed to be sharps, or middlings, to supplement the swill from what was known as 'the wash tub'. What a mixture went into that barrel, often a hogshead cider barrel. Potato peelings, apple cores and peelings, rotten fruit, parsnips, washing-up water, the water from the cooking of greens and potatoes – the whole fermented into a mixture, a smelly concoction under a grey scum.

The cottager scooped out with a handled bowl half a bucket full and leavened it with balancer meal. Pigs thrived on it, they grew fat on it. If a pig club was in credit at the end of the year the funds were divided among the members. If, as in one case I knew, a pig almost fit for the butcher died of sunstroke and the member was compensated, that was a loss to the club.

Besides the swill tub pigs thrive on greenstuff. Cottagers fed swill twice a day but at dinner-time the spoilt pet at the bottom of the garden had fresh cabbage greens, anything in season, and a shovel full of slack coal to keep him in good health.

From Easter until Christmas approached the family fed the pig. It grew, and the neighbours guessed the weight in scores of pounds. A good bacon pig would be 15 score, an extra special one 20 score. When the day arrived for the pig killer to come and butcher the cottagers' pigs, it was a day of drama for the whole family. Hopefully the children were at school, and the wives took the train to town, away from the slaughter. Either Laughing Tom or Joe Whittle would kill maybe three pigs for neighbours in a day. Pigs do squeal on their way to the pig bench, but the end is quick as Tom or Joe did the necessary.

In Tibblestone and around the scalding of pigs is a foreign way. Here, the bristles were burnt off with a bolting of straw lit at one end and carefully scattered with a small hay fork as the flames took the bristles from the carcass. After came the buckets of hot and cold water, the scrubbing brush, the bass broom, until the carcass was clean and white. The butcher then took out the belly, the chittlings, the liver and lights. Then the pig was hung on hooks to the ceiling of an outhouse to set, and cut up the next day.

There is some mystique surrounding pig killing. Neighbours would give away some liver or offal when the pig was killed and would expect a return gift when the pig next door was made into bacon. It was considered bad manners to take the empty dish which had held the offal back washed and clean. Women were not allowed to touch the flitches of bacon as they cured in the brine. If a woman had a period at that time it was said that the bacon would go bad. No doubt the flitches of bacon, called pictures, on the walls of cottage kitchens were valuable for survival but so much folklore existed. It was said that if a pig was killed when the moon waned the bacon would fry away in the pan . . . I wonder.

THE DOCTOR AND THE VET

In these last days of the twentieth century the powers that be are advising families that when they have minor illnesses they should do as our ancestors did – treat the case at home. Seventy years ago, before the days of antibiotics, folk relied more on remedies handed down from their mothers and fathers. The Doctor's waiting-room is a thing of today.

What were the various treatments for the common cold in the Tibblestone of old? Eucalyptus taken on lumps of sugar, on handkerchiefs; gargling for sore throats with permanganate of potash in warm water; hot cider for coughs; camphorated oil on the chest on brown paper and stitched to the vest; onion gruel at bedtime, and a concoction known as kettle broth, which was dry toast in a basin of hot water and butter with salt and pepper; linseed and liquorice drink, with boiled linseed and sticks of liquorice dissolved into the mixture, which, when cold, formed a jelly-like liquid pleasant to drink. This latter concoction was a remedy for colds on the chest, along with goose grease rubbed on the chest.

Home treatment did help the Doctor's practice. He was free to visit the more serious cases, and prescribed linseed poultices for congestion of the chest.

Of course, not everything could be successfully treated at home. Often pneumonia was a killer before penicillin became available. The dread influenza epidemic of 1919 is said to have killed more folk than the Great War. I never knew where Dad got the idea of preventing flu germs from invading our farm house, but he had his way of disinfecting the rooms, something I have never seen done before or since. He took a coal shovel of red hot embers and from a blue bottle marked POISON, he sprinkled carbolic acid on the embers and blew the fumes into every part of the house, including the bedrooms. It was supposed to ward off the flu, but we all went down with it.

Most families had a medicine chest stocked with the treatments of the day. Iodine for cuts and grazed knees, boracic powder and the pink boracic lint which stuck to the wound like glue! Doctor's advised oiled silk to prevent the dressing from sticking. I remember how it healed the angry arm I had after a vaccination.

Men on the land made their own embrocation for what they called rheumatics – a mixture of turpentine, linseed oil and beaten eggs – but most folk resorted to Sloan's Liniment, or Elliman's Embrocation, or Winter Green Ointment. The smell of Winter Green and eucalyptus brings back memories of Chapel on winter evenings.

In the draughty cottages and farm houses the younger members of the family did suffer from chilblains. In centrally-heated houses of today one rarely hears of this painful malady. George, our under carter, told me one remedy. 'Put your feet in the chamber pot,' he said. I got into trouble for that, but the woman who did our washing recommended boiling ivy leaves in a saucepan and bathing the feet in the mixture, and that did work.

Apparently a remedy for most ills can be found in the fields and hedgerows. That little plant with a yellow flower called Agrimony used to grow on the Hill. Tea made from this herb is said to help with water trouble. I have picked the leaves and flowers and taken it to Shepherd Tidmarsh when he was ill with water problems.

Senna pods, Cascara Sagrada, and Caster Oil kept the organs working when they were sluggish, otherwise grated acorns for diarrhoea was an old remedy. I wonder, did Brimstone and Treacle clear the blood? It was somewhat anti-social!

It's a long time since Dr Edward Roberson rode his horse through the lanes and fields of Tibblestone. His medicines were basic. He had one special mixture for those who over-indulged at Christmas, and another one for the members of The Club who celebrated Trinity Monday too well. The Doctor always made a note of the date of Trinity Monday Club Feast. It seemed that nine months after those celebrations the Doctor always had a busy time with a spate of births in Tibblestone.

One piece of advice, I remember, was given with all Dr Roberson's medicines. 'Always give the mixture a thundering good shake', the Doctor would instruct as he handed over the sealing-waxed and white-paper-covered bottle.

As the Doctor's workload has increased today so has that of the Vet. Veterinary surgeons were wholly for the treatment of horses at the turn of the century. Cow doctors with experience of animals attended ailing cattle. It's very different today. The Vet's life is often a mixture of treating all sorts of animals, from farm animals to pets of all descriptions, from parrots to guinea pigs.

Looking back over Tibblestone the Vet came from Tewkesbury. Laughing Tom, a very talented cow doctor, had his ways with animals when they were ill. Cows which lost their cud were treated with a mixture of the liquid from fat bacon boiled in cabbages. Before the salves were on the market chapped cows' udders were treated with fresh liquor, that is unsalted lard. Most animals were treated without a call from the vet. Cottagers who had a dog under par noticed the animal eating grass and gave it a dose of Benbows Mixture or Bob Martin's Condition Powder. Chickens from late hatched broods which had a condition known as gapes were treated with turpentine, administered with a feather on to the bird's tongue.

Shepherd Tidmarsh castrated our lambs in a way which had been done for generations. I helped him in the Old Cross Barn and thought nothing, as a boy in my teens, of the primitive surgery. I held the lamb against my chest, holding its four legs. The shepherd cut off the end of the lamb's purse with his bone-handled shut-knife exposing the testicles. He leant forward, grasping the testicles with his few teeth and when the cord holding them broke he spat them into a bucket. With the juice of chewed tobacco Alf Tidmarsh spat into the open wound.

This whiskered man with blood on his chin was not a pretty sight, but something accepted by master and man. Dad and his partner bought the twist tobacco for him. Shepherd Tidmarsh made a meal with lambs' sweetbreads and the tails, which he docked with a knife.

The elasticator, an Australian invention, a simple rubber band, has replaced the old way of castration. I have used this method, which is a great step forward and less painful.

A scourge among young lambs in the pre-antibiotic age was dysentery. It killed hundreds of lambs, a diarrhoea ending in a pneumonia. Thanks to veterinary research, today's vaccinations have eliminated this killer. What the shepherd called wool in the gullet among lambs was nothing of the kind. The lambs were dying, at a week or so old, with pulpy kidney disease. Thankfully, this is now controlled by a vaccine too. I have spent hours collecting the wool caught on sheep troughs after being told that the lambs will get it in their maw and die. Pulpy kidney disease had not been discovered then.

When calves were bought in the market and were suckled by another cow often the calf would scour with the change of milk. This could be remedied by giving the calf less milk and using one of the powders of the day. Raw eggs were also considered a good medicine. The infectious calf diarrhoea was often fatal in those days, but modern veterinary science has controlled this problem today.

I had a calf with white scour in a bad condition lying on a straw bed, unable even to stand. A farmer friend said to me, as we met in the market, 'Go and see Mr Smith the Pershore Chemist. Take a bottle with you and he will give you a marvellous medicine.'

Mr Smith gave me a pint bottle of liquid smelling of chloridine and peppermint; he charged me 4s. I gave the calf a dose at dinner-time, another at tea-time and again at bed-time. The next morning I was expecting the worst as I opened the door of the calf pen, but that calf met me at the door! What Mr Smith's remedy was I'll never know; he certainly had a good name for medicine, human and animal.

CHAPTER NINETEEN

FROM MAGIC LANTERNS
TO TELEVISION

In the Tibblestone villages entertainment was different to today's activities, but there was still a variety to be found. When the social life in Tibblestone in the late nineteenth century and early in the twentieth is considered, it's often only the pub that is thought of, but there was so much more than just that old drinking establishment with its curious ancient notices: 'As a bird is known by his note so is a man known by his conversation. Swearing strictly prohibited. Signed John Cresswell.' The Victorians did attempt in Tibblestone to keep to a code of conduct. Card playing, dominoes, quoits were permitted for six days a week, but on Sundays there were no games played in the pubs.

Several times during the winter evenings the Recreation Room, an Army hut from the First World War, was filled. A lantern lecture was being given by the British and Foreign Bible Society. Picture the scene on a cold night: an Army hut lit by a row of swinging oil lamps, a coke stove red hot, with a group of us boys sitting on a bench under a window. The atmosphere was anything but pure, with the smell of drying corduroy from the farm labourers. The fact was that it was warm and dark, and from our bench there was a good view of the magic lantern screen.

Percy Wigley, an ex-engineer from Birmingham, a brother-in-law of Parson Baker, operated the lantern, which was powered by acetylene gas. The carbide in the container had a drip of water, which constantly produced gas through a rubber pipe to the jet on the lantern. The light was quite brilliant compared with the paraffin lamps of the day.

A missionary had arrived from Burma, where he had been proclaiming the Christian Gospel. He was staying in the village, probably with Mr Bernard Nicklin, who chaired the meeting and provided the magic lantern. We started off by singing 'The Church's One Foundation'. This gave both the Anglican Church and the Chapel common ground. In fact the folk from the Chapel patronized these lectures more than the Anglicans. The words of the hymn were shown on the screen, a poor black and white imitation of the Hymn Book, but we sang and Bunch Baldwyn played the piano.

The missionary stressed the plight of the folk in the far-flung part of the British Empire. The first pictures, in blurred black and white, were of the giraffe-necked women of Burma. They apparently had bands of beads around their necks giving them a giraffe appearance. These women and girls in straw skirts were topless, and we boys, fixing our eyes on black boobs, stifled a laugh. This was the pièce de résistance. In the 1920s we never saw any coloured people in the village, or in the whole of the Tibblestone. But to see topless females, that was something. Perhaps the whole point of the lecture was to support the missionary, but here our education was furthered. We had seen something hitherto barred from public view.

A man, smartly dressed in breeches and leggings, took up a collection. Mr Nicklin thanked the missionary. Percy Wigley put a final hymn on the screen. This time the words were the right way up – they weren't always!

As we sang 'Lord Dismiss Us with Thy Blessing' Percy had turned too much water onto the carbide. The flame enveloped the lantern, it caught fire. It was soon put out, but an incident such as this was just a part of the evening's entertainment for the boys.

When the pantomime took place there were lots of preparations to construct a stage of sorts. The billiard table provided part of the platform. The scenery at the back, painted by a decorator from Grafton, gave the game away that the performance was Dick Whittington and his Cat. Maggie, a rather masculine sixteen-year-old, took the part of the cat and a local farm bailiff was Dick Whittington. Oh, the curtains always jammed between the acts, the oil lamps gave shadows where shadows were not needed, there was lots of prompting, but everyone had a good laugh. Amateur but sometimes so funny, and even more so when it was not meant to be.

Armistice Day was always a day of remembrance. The War Memorial in Portland stone was inscribed with the names of the men who had given their lives for their country, an inscription which struck one as just right. The words above the names of the men can be mused over time and time again. They read:

> These Men were a Wall unto Us
> By Night and by Day.

On Armistice Day a service was held at the Memorial. Men who had been part of that wall marched from the Cross to the Memorial. A proud lot of countrymen with their medals swinging from the lapels of their jackets, like martingales do on cart horses; a few wore bowler hats. The band from Tewkesbury, dressed in cast-off uniforms of the St John Ambulance, played one tune – it was always 'Colonel Bogey'.

In the afternoon the wives and widows of ex-servicemen were busy in the Recreation Room preparing the Armistice Tea. Mrs Cresswell and Mrs Ellis organized this feast of ham off the bone, of trifles, blancmanges and cakes of all description. Meanwhile, little Reggie Nind, with his very red beard, was carrying buckets of water from a stand-pipe in our yard for making the tea in two great urns. The ex-servicemen sat together at a long trestle table. The evening was free for them I believe, others paid 1s 6d.

Mr J.C. Nicklin, Landowner and Farmer, from The Close, took the chair at the impromptu concert. Very little had been planned, yet everything always fell into place. The piano belonged to the village school; it had been brought down to what we called 'The Rooms' by a porter from the station on a four-wheeled truck. There were some good singers who entertained during the evening. Ewart Morrison, a smart ex-Army Officer, dressed in a navy pin-striped suit, sang with feeling 'Trumpeter, What Are You Sounding Now?'

Miss Cotton played the piano. More rustic songs came from Jack Langley, who had done some work as a game keeper. His tenor rendering of 'The Lincolnshire Poacher' was applauded by everyone. 'Tom Bowling' followed, a tear-jerker. Mother sang 'Keep the Home Fires Burning'. She had taken singing lessons from someone named Lombardini.

John Ellis, painter and decorator, a member of the Church choir, had brought with him a stack of music, all ballads. His deep bass voice was lubricated continuously by a dish of jelly and blancmange balanced on top of the piano. When Mrs Cresswell from the shop sang 'My Old Man said Follow the Van, and Don't Dilly Dally on the Way' there was a touch of the Old Kent Road, Cockney-flavoured.

Tom Barnett, thatcher, needed no piano to accompany 'The Beautiful Picture in the Beautiful Golden Frame'. His rendition of 'If Those Lips Could only Speak' was sung with such feeling that the concert hall was hushed. Tom was a man and a half, who had fought in Salonica, worked on farms in Canada, and thatched most of the cottages in the village.

When Mr Nicklin's health failed, Dad chaired the Armistice Tea. He had difficulty in persuading Alf Tidmarsh, our shepherd, to sing, but after a few pokes in the ribs from his little wife he sang:

> The fox and the hare,
> The badger and the bear,
> And the birds in the greenwood tree.
> The pretty little rabbit, so engaging in his habit,
> They all have a mate but me.

One verse went like this:

> She was sixteen stone
> All muscle and bone,
> She looked at me with an awful leer.
> I thought she was mine, but she fell into a decline,
> Through swallowing a mouse in her beer.

William Sandford didn't trust the notes on the piano, which had been shaken and rattled all down the street. He brought with him a tuning fork. Miss Cotton played the accompaniment of 'The Campbells are Coming and a Ho'. He explained that he and the pianist had only got a line between them, sheet music being on the scarce side. This brought a question from the Captain of the cricket team, C.K., a natural comedian, a man who had fought the Turks in the Middle East: 'Mr Sandford, what are you and Miss Cotton going to do on washing day?'

William Sandford replied, 'What's that got to do with singing?'

'Well, Mr Sandford, you have only got a line between you and Miss Cotton.'

I don't think this pleased the tenor, who launched into 'The Campbells are Coming'.

The whole village was at the concert, and the lamp light in a smoke-filled room gave shadows, and men lived their experiences over again. The evening ended with 'Auld Lang Syne'. There has never been such a galaxy of mixed entertainment as happened on Armistice Night in an Army hut in the 1920s.

Whist Drives in the Recreation Room in the twenties were well patronized. Around Christmas they were called Fur and Feather Drives, prizes being pheasants, partridges, rabbits and hares. Well I remember the players coming back past our farm house on those dark winter nights, their little candle lanterns casting a glow of fairy lights into the bedroom window, their voices chattering of their luck that evening, and most of all, the thump of Albert's wooden leg. Its regular thump on the road sounded quite eerie to me.

A strict rule of meetings at the Recreation Room was that no alcohol was to be consumed on the premises.

'We are not standing for that ruling,' Pedlar Palmer and Harry Attwood declared to the whist players.

'Smacks of the Chapel,' Pedlar said. 'Two of the committee members are strict Chapel.'

However, under the wooden floor of the Recreation Room there was ample room for bottles of beer. Those who fancied a drink at the interval drank their beer in what some called the Vestibule, others the Vestry of the hut, so side-stepping the rule of no alcohol on the premises itself. This Recreation Room has long since gone, and one thing that came to light when the building was demolished was the amount of beer bottles under the floor. Names of breweries which are but a memory were still visible on those bottles – Sladden and Collier, Little Chelt, Rowlands, to name but a few.

Sometimes the Whist Drive was followed by a dance, a band from Winchcombe provided the music. One of the lady members gave dancing lessons to the girls of Tibblestone. One local market gardener said, 'If the girls learn to dance there will soon be some bastard kids. My daughter's not going.' Sad to say this youngster was the only one of the girls who had a 'love child'.

Previously, at the turn of the century, dances were held in the Ball Room at Old Manor Farm. Later on, these were well organized in the room over the Nag Stables. In the stables below, Jim Vale, the under carter, looked after the suitors' horses. Music there was provided by the village orchestra, a little group which played at Church and at village fêtes.

The Beckford hand-bell ringers were a group who performed at social evenings in the Tibblestone. A lot of the members were named Smith. Children's parties known as 'Bun Struggles' took place at Christmas, and the pensioners had their annual rabbit pie supper at the New Year. Well-meaning amateur cooks spoilt the pies one year. Cooking the rabbits before the pies were baked was said to be unnecessary by those who knew it all but the result was half-cooked meat in the pies.

Sometimes I think back and wonder whatever did we do on winter evenings before the wireless and television occupied that corner of the living-room? However, in the Tibblestone villages there was entertainment aplenty to keep us all amused.

CHAPTER TWENTY

TIBBLESTONE FUNERALS

The villagers of Tibblestone all had that secret dread of leaving this world but were convinced of an afterlife in a better land. Men and women living close to the land and seeing the seasons of the year, the falling of the leaves from the trees, the death of animals, had a real instinct of eternal life, looking forward to re-birth and spring. To even doubt the existence of God was maybe thought, but never spoken.

George Palmer, a gardener from Paris, that little hamlet on Bredon edge, was an atheist, a Communist, and very much against royalty. It took some courage in a Conservative, Anglican community to take that stand. George had consumption, or TB. Some said it was a smoker's cough and were afraid he wouldn't recover. I knew George through Dad's partner, Harry Bailey, who tolerated this thorn in the flesh to the righteous and holy. I went rabbiting with George and Harry on Saturday afternoons. This man from Paris kept good gun dogs, was an excellent shot, and kept hutches of ferrets. Apart from rabbits the only thing which he had in common with Harry Bailey was that he taught him to drive a Studebaker car. I imagine they never discussed religion or politics.

George Palmer eventually died and the shortest way to bring his body down to the village road was through Harry Bailey's orchard at Old Manor Farm. There was a so-called law that to take a corpse across a field constituted a right of way. Harry was worried, he had had problems before with folks taking a short cut to Paris through his orchard. George Palmer's body eventually took the official road, down Bakers Lane. I don't recall his funeral but knowing him the body never entered the Church.

When I was a boy, death and burial were looked upon very differently in a village. Gray in his *Elegy* expressed well the feelings of inevitability felt by the men of the land.

> The curfew tolls the knell of parting day,
> The lowing herd winds slowly o'er the lea,
> The ploughman homeward plods his weary way,
> And leaves the world to darkness and to me.

> Beneath those rugged elms, that yew tree's shade,
> Where heaves the turf in many a mould'ring heap,
> Each in his narrow cell for ever laid,
> The rude forefathers of the hamlet sleep.

> Oft did the harvest to their sickle yield,
> Their furrow oft the stubborn glebe has broke;
> How jocund did they drive their team afield!
> How bow'd the woods beneath their sturdy stroke!

> Some Village-Hampden that with dauntless breast
> The little tyrant of his fields withstood;
> Some mute inglorious Milton here may rest,
> Some Cromwell guiltless of his Country's blood.

> Far from the madding crowd's ignoble strife
> Their sober wishes never learn'd to stray;
> Along the cool sequester'd Vale of Life
> They kept the noiseless tenor of their way.

> Haply some hoary-headed swain may say,
> 'Oft have we seen him at the peep of dawn
> 'Brushing with hasty steps the dews away
> 'To meet the sun upon the upland lawn.'

'One morn I miss'd him on the custom'd hill,
'Along the heath, and near his fav'rite tree;
'Another came; nor yet beside the rill,
'Nor up the lawn, nor at the wood was he.

'The next with dirges due in sad array
'Slow thro' the Church-way path we saw him borne.
'Approach and read (for thou can'st read) the lay,
'Grav'd on the stone beneath yon aged thorn.'

The Epitaph
Here rests his Head upon the Lap of Earth
A Youth to Fortune and to Fame unknown;
Fair Science frown'd not on his humble birth,
And melancholy mark'd him for her own.
Large was his Bounty, and his Soul sincere,
Heav'n did a Recompense as largely send;
He gave to Mis'ry all he had, a Tear;
He gain'd from Heav'n ('twas all he wish'd) a Friend,
No farther seek his Merits to disclose,
Or draw his Frailties from their dread Abode,
(There they alike in trembling Hope repose)
The Bosom of his Father and his God.

Thomas Gray, *Elegy written in a Country Church-Yard*, 1751

Charlie Moore, Sexton of the Church, captain of the bell ringers, passed the bell on the death of villagers. There were so many rings on the death of a man, some fewer for a woman. As a boy this mournful exercise of Mr Moore's sent shivers down my spine. The funeral a few days later was even more macabre.

If the villager had relatives a distance away they were informed with a letter in a black-edged envelope. The sight of these did nothing to soften the blow of the loss. It seems that the bier used for carrying the coffin and kept at Beckford Church was used for other village funerals in the Tibblestone. What a work of art this four-wheeled carriage was, built by a coach builder and wheelwright from oak, stained light brown with wooden-spoked wheels. Ponto fetched the bier from Beckford. Crossed in love as a young man, he lived in a cart shed, worked at boys' jobs on the land, leading horses, scaring birds. He was a little bent man, pulling the empty vehicle along Beckford Way to the cottage where the man lay in a coffin in the front room. The four bearers were not undertaker's men but men of the village who carried at funerals, a final gesture to the family of the deceased.

As the little procession came down the village street, quiet apart from the creaking of the bier, every blind, every curtain was drawn. It is strange that today the expression 'curtains' means the inevitable (death). I must admit to peeping from behind the curtain of our farm house. The coffin on the bier was covered with garden flowers, no cellophane wreaths from town, wallflowers, daffodils in spring, chrysanthemums in autumn.

Behind the bearers and the creaking vehicle the mourners walked all in black. If Dad was going to pay his respects he followed behind as the procession passed our gate. The black suit with high lapels, cloth buttons and his bowler hat, which all looked aged, seemed the uniform of the others who followed.

In the Church Bunch Baldwyn pulled out all the stops when she played 'The Dead March in Saul'. Parson Baker, after 'Abide With Me', then spoke of the brother departed. If ever a man deserved the OBE it was Parson Baker. His addresses at funerals were something to remember. With pursed lips and great thought Wilson Baker made some lovely little references to the person who had died; whatever the character he always found something special, a little gem, to say.

Shakespeare's words 'The evil that men do lives after them/The good is often buried with their bones' were contradicted in a nice way by Parson Baker. There was a dignity about the working man of the land, a fear of the workhouse, and of having to be buried by the Parish. Two sick men I knew paid a penny a week insurance for their funeral. Things have changed and with huge populations in towns and cities and graveyards becoming full, cremation is the alternative to burials. This can be dignified, but somehow a picture of queues of mourners waiting their turn, a sort of pipeline, is conjured up, making the issue of life and death appear somewhat cheap.

It's a changed world now and it is true that perhaps the mourning and black of yesteryear were overdone. I remember seeing a chap in a black cap pitching boltings of straw behind the threshing machine; he had lost his sister. He probably felt better for remembering her in this way; black bands around the arms of men's jackets were common, and were worn for so long.

Life doesn't seem so precious today, but perhaps this is because we are too often exposed to the carnage of war, of famine, through pictures on the television. There is the temptation to 'eat, drink and be merry, for tomorrow we die'. The Church is struggling to convince this generation of life everlasting. It all seemed easier when men followed the plough, worked the allotment, lived close to the land.

CHAPTER TWENTY-ONE

THOMAS WILLIAM ARCHER

U pon the death of Mr Harry Bailey my father, Tom Archer, came to possess the manorial rights at Ashton under Hill, but he never occupied the Manor. He farmed the land, reared and fattened the half-bred Hereford cattle, ran a flock of Kerry Hill sheep, marketed the fruit and vegetables from the fields until his health gave way at the beginning of the war.

My brother, Thomas William, then farmed the Old Manor and moved with his family into the farm house. He was a progressive man. When he took over the Old Manor Farm and became Lord of the Manor he did extensive restoration work on the house, a house of great antiquity. The house was kept a replica of the Baldwyn's period and tastefully restored, and Connie, his wife, gave Thomas William six children. He was a practical man, but found time for some recreation. He was a superb shot with a twelve-bore gun, once downing two deer with a left and right barrel, in those days before it became illegal to shoot deer with shotguns.

A staunch Nonconformist and an able local preacher, as Secretary of the village Chapel he also engaged eminent preachers from farther afield than Tibblestone itself. A pillar of the Chapel, Thomas William never worked on Sundays. He never smoked or drank alcohol, but could always be seen in the fields with his workers, usually eating an apple. The Tibblestone Hundred was important to him; in his lifetime he collected local history and above all others was able to present his knowledge at the Parish Council and School Board.

Thomas William's approach to farming and market gardening was very different from his late father. Whereas his father was a careful business man, brought up the son of a smallholder, he had prospered in the days of depression partly because of his thrift and his lifestyle.

Thomas William had an uncanny instinct for what to plant, when to plant, and how to market his crops. He lashed out with new machinery, irrigation systems, a risk which his father would never have taken. Tom bought second-hand tools for working the farm, never bought a new tractor. Thomas William invested in every useful implement produced by the agricultural engineers.

As the plums ripened in the orchard alongside the Beckford Road, planted by Tom in the 1920s, the fruit had always been carefully picked and marketed in chips. Thomas William took over in 1940 when the war was raging. He soon contracted with canners and jam-makers for the fruit his men picked. Pershore Plums, hard and green for the canners. Things had changed and the change suited Thomas William.

During the war apples more than 1½ inches in diameter had a ready sale regardless of the variety or flavour. No imports from abroad made a difference. With modern equipment and sprays which produced clean fruit, Thomas William's apples and plums were eagerly sought by the local Co-operative Society and all-comers. The land responded to his farming as it had never done before, the reasons being good cultivation with modern machinery and unstinting dressings of fertilizer. The plum trees, free from aphis and caterpillar, smiled in spring as the bees from hives brought in from the Cotswolds gave a continual hum at Old Manor Farm.

Here was a happy place where a staff of eight or nine men and a dozen women produced crops par excellence. Diddycoys and gentlemen of the road found work with Thomas William in the fields in summer. He never advertised for labour and kept some of his father's workers on as pensioners.

Thomas William was not a stock farmer but did buy cattle from Hereford Market to fatten in the straw yards. Old Bill Spires looked after the stock as if it was his own and some pretty good beef came from the Manor. The farmyard manure from the Herefords produced crops of runner beans and peas on the farm, providing work for twelve women picking the crops.

Tons of produce went by lorry to the Co-operative market of Littleton and Badsey Growers, known as LBG. Thomas William became Vice President of the Society, following in the footsteps of C.H. Binyan, a brother of the poet. He, like his father, was a shrewd committee man and had his way in a quiet unassuming manner.

As one Christmas Day followed another, work at the Old Manor proceeded in a pattern. The young Squire had kept a diary since his youth but now that diary was an important part of the working of the farm. Autumn-sown sprout seed, sown in August, the plants set in rows 3 feet wide and 3 feet apart, produced a crop in the following August and September. The exact date of sowing the seed gathered from the diary was vital. By planting Seville beans on 1 November, the crop was harvested the following June. Round-seeded Early Bird peas drilled at Candlemas were picked in June. Wrinkled varieties such as Onwards, Kelvedon Wonder, Lincolns produced a succession of peas throughout the summer. So Thomas William's records, often quoted to neighbours, constituted a charter for market gardens.

After 1945 eating habits changed, the meat and two vegetables for Sunday dinner was not the ritual it had been. Families with cars went to the seaside, they picnicked on salads, and ready-roasted broiler chickens. As the demand for the old vegetables declined, lettuce and spring onions took their place. Salads were eaten all the year round. Thomas William then grew these crops and large acreages of sage and parsley, herbs for the pâtés, the chickens and so on. In fact he introduced a new variety of sage named after him. He made it less labour intensive, cutting the herbs with a tractor and flail mower.

So the Tibblestone appearance changed from the run of the mill vegetables which had been its image for generations to herbs and salad crops in large acreages. Over at Beckford the big glasshouse of Messrs Woodward produced tons of tomatoes, and they also grew exotic fruits native to the sub-tropics.

The old style of harvesting the corn was disappearing fast. Combine harvesters were replacing the binders, and corn ricks became a rarity. The corn fields at the Old Manor soon resounded with the hum of the combines and the pathetic drone of threshing machines was but a memory. Ken Pratt, a very skilled tractor driver, was soon sitting on the deck of the massive combine cutting and threshing the corn. The machine worked through the night with the young Squire at the helm. Neighbours anxious to harvest in one operation were soon having their crops dealt with on contract by Thomas William. The ricks of hay which had for so long been a part of Tibblestone's landscape became a rarity as Thomas William's pick-up baler made a tidy job in the hay field.

One skill of this young farmer was his ability to work out piece-work rates for his workers. His method was to get the best from the men and women, allowing them to sometimes double their wages. So much for picking apples, plums, etc., and rates for hoeing by the acre or the row, planting by the thousand plants, all very well thought out. The workers were satisfied as a rule and were listened to if the rate didn't give them room to improve their hourly pay. 'What's the rate for sprout planting?' the farmer was so often asked by neighbours, who went back to their men saying, 'That's what Thomas William is paying, he's never far out.'

So this part of Tibblestone Hundred thrived under Thomas William, who employed a gang of workers the like of which would never be seen again. 'Labour intensive' is a modern phrase, but the folk of Ashton under Hill had, I think, the privilege of working on the land in rain or shine for a good master. Automation was on the way, but Thomas William kept his staff, and the crops came from the land every week of the year.

When his father, Tom Archer, farmed the Old Manor with Harry Bailey the growing and marketing of vegetable was very different. In a dry summer it became difficult to grow sprouts and cabbage but these two men never gave up. With a cider barrel of water from the brook, men and women with buckets and cocoa cans watered the plants as the sun bore down and made the land like a desert. This continual process, giving every sprout plant water from cocoa cans, kept the crop alive but Harry and Tom knew that there would be a shortage of sprouts the following winter. So, years of shortages followed years of glut, but it was all part of the pattern.

In those days Nitrate of Lime came in barrels from Norway. A mystical chemical, it turned to a watery solution when exposed to the air. The women workers on the farm put a small handful of this magic fertilizer to each plant and the men covered it with their hands. In a few days the plants sent their fibrous roots to the damp soil and fed on that Nitrate of Lime. With a reduced acreage of sprouts, the price in the market was good. During a hard winter sprouts were like gold-dust in the shops. Men picked in snow and frost, glad of the money as the piece-work rate was doubled.

Thomas William knew the value of irrigation. He had the Moat Pond near the Church as a reservoir for irrigating his crops. No cider barrels, no cocoa cans but an electric motor which pumped the spring water off Bredon Hill nearly to Grafton. The parsley, the sage, the spring onions, thrived because of this irrigation, while his neighbour's wilted in the sun.

Days of big prices for sprouts were over. In the winter now, there were ample vegetables in the deep freeze. I remember the winter of 1962/3 when the greenstuff was killed by frost and what remained was eaten by pigeons. But then the pigeons died of hunger. Thomas William had a crop of Borecole, Curly Kale, that alone survived. He always had something to market. It's an old adage in market gardening – 'Always plant more after a year of bad prices'. Some got disheartened and reduced their acreage, but it's all swings and roundabouts.

Thomas William, after ploughing in crops, planted again the next year, but in times of change he was always a jump in front of his neighbours. When floods of imported fruit came from abroad he was ruthless, bulldozing his older trees and planting barley.

It's sad that Thomas William, who, as one of his workers said, never abused himself, died after a short illness. He was buried on the new piece of land given to the Church by him as owner, and by me who tenanted the land. Together we met the Bishop of Gloucester who dedicated the new churchyard. A great change came over Ashton under Hill on his death, and that of that other stalwart of the Church, James Bernard Nicklin. These men had a feel for the land and the ordinary folk of the village, a fertile part of Tibblestone.

CHAPTER TWENTY TWO

CHARLES ARCHER, PRESENT LORD OF THE MANOR OF ASHTON UNDER HILL

O n the death of Thomas William in 1976 young Charles Archer became Lord of the Manor. At the time he lived in Tythe Court, a section of the farm where the Tythe Court Barn had been used to store produce that was due to the Vicar, his tenth of the crop grown on Old Manor Farm. A little while after Thomas William's death, Charles and his wife, Lesley, and family moved into the Manor House.

Because of competition from abroad, the growing of fruit at Tibblestone had become precarious. The growers who survived operated the Pick-Your-Own system of marketing. Thomas William had seen this approaching and uprooted most of the apple and plum trees. Charles inherited a mixture of corn fields, as well as acres and acres of sage and parsley for drying at the local Co-operative. He had taken his father's place on the committee there.

It was quite a daunting situation for the young man. Fortunately Lesley, his wife, shared the organization, paper work, and so on. Together they won an award for conservation and the little estate bristled with trees, and headlands left for fauna and flora.

Charles trained at Hartpury Agricultural College and this stood him in good stead when he took over from his late father. Like Thomas William, Charles' heart is in the land but not in livestock. Some of the hill land at this Tibblestone farm has been let to a neighbour for cattle and sheep grazing.

During the first years of his farming, Charles inherited quite a large labour force on his 200-odd acres. The system of growing runner beans up sticks for market gave casual work to a dozen women from the village, and the sage growing entailed so much hand work by his men, in the constant war against weeds, that change was inevitable – the farm was too labour intensive.

The sage and parsley have been scrapped for fields of wheat and barley, and the labour force reduced to a minimum. Fields of spring onions, kept weed-free by spraying, grow from Christmas Day to Christmas Day. Spinach has become a cash crop along with beetroot. Rationalization of Old Manor Farm took an inevitable turn.

It is a sad fact of life that the medium-sized farm has become difficult to remain economical. Some of Charles' neighbours reduced their workforce, venturing on the Pick-Your-Own system in the fruit orchards. This did not appeal to Charles and Lesley Archer. For one thing, the orchards had gone and there was little incentive to replant. Another fact was that the Pick-Your-Own system entailed Sunday work. Sundays are something special to the family, with Charles the Secretary of the Free Church.

Alongside the Manor House a substantial brick building had been erected by Squire Baldwyn early in the nineteenth century. It consisted of what was known as the Nag Stable, where Jim Dance the old groom, tended the Baldwyn stud of hunters. The stable was well appointed, with water laid on to the stalls, the walls tiled in cream and gold. Adjoining the stable a groom's bothy with a fireplace made excellent accommodation for a horse man. The room adjacent was for fodder, walled off to a trap house where Harry Bailey kept his Governess car. A staircase led to what was known as the Ballroom. Here, in the pre-village hall days, dances were held in Squire Baldwyn's time. Dates were fixed at the full moon every month, the young farmers and the farmers' daughters took advantage of the moonlight to dance the night away.

Charles and Lesley have converted the ground floor of the stable into holiday accommodation. The middle room where Squire Baldwyn stored fodder for his hunters had been important in Squire Harry Bailey's time. This professional market gardener grew acres of asparagus, and the room became known as the Gras House. As the men cut the gras from the beds in Beckfords Way, women tied it in bundles with raffia and Mr Harry Bailey put four bundles together to form a hundred of gras, tied with withy sticks from the brook side. Here the women also tied the spring onions in bunches, earning a penny a dozen for these, and Harry Bailey tied a dozen together with withies. The place reeked of history, the smell of onions, the scent of gras.

No doubt when Charles did the conversion he found relics of its past use, a place of work where the whole village in this Hundred of Tibblestone was involved. Squire Baldwyn's nag stable is now a suitably furnished sitting-room, the bothy a well-appointed kitchen. Charles stores wheat and barley in the ballroom, a room which will always remind me of wedding receptions and social evenings, and the sound of men on wet days threshing sprout seed and wallflower seed with pegs.

The saw pit has gone, as has the old bull pen, a place where Squire Baldwyn kept his white shorthorn bull, tempting his neighbours to go in to the savage beast. The cart horse stable is free of those lovely Shires and is used to store chemical sprays to keep the crops free of weeds.

But Charles is so unlike Squire Baldwyn or Squire Harry Bailey. No one ever argued that Squire Baldwyn was eccentric, yet he had a sense of humour, a dry sense of humour. When he asked Jim Dance if he wanted anything for the stable from town, Jim replied, 'Yes Sir, some soft soap.'

The Squire thought a minute before he replied, 'Ah. There's a lot of that used round here.'

It's said that young men have visions, old men dream dreams. Harry Bailey was not a mild man, working for him was exacting, but he treated me like a son. I can picture him now, coming from his kitchen on a winter's morning stripped to shirt sleeves, the yard rock solid with frost. The gate slams, he calls, 'Ralph, Ralph.'

The carter appears with a square kerf of clover on his head, like a mattress, on his way from the rick to the stable.

'Ralph, just be careful with the clover. It's a long while to May Day.'

Ralph, with eyebrows raised, replies from under his load, 'That's alright, Master, but my horses have got to have their fittle.'

Harry Bailey didn't know that Ralph had raided the granary for cattle cake to give to Boxer, his favourite chestnut gelding.

George comes, whistling across the yard. 'My goy, Master Bailey, it's putting it together this morning. The ground's as hard as a rock.'

Harry answers, 'It's not cold, George. Feel my hands.'

George, in his usual Shakespearean style, counters, 'It's alright for you, you have got an undervest on like a sheep skin.'

And they both laugh, for despite his being stripped to his shirt sleeves he did wear a flannelette undershirt down to his knees.

'Now Fred,' the Boss turns to me, 'I want you along with me today ferreting the big holt in Boss Close. Fetch a couple of ferrets from their box at the back of the Bull Pen. Bring that black and white Fitcher for one.'

I gingerly picked two of the pink-eyed creatures and put them in a sack bag with some hay in the bottom, meeting Mr Harry by the Bramley apple trees. He carried a graft, a long-bladed spade. We ferreted the holt, driving the rabbits into what Harry called a spout, dug down where Jum his Italian greyhound was scratching. Mr Harry lay on the grass and listened. 'There's traffic under here. Start and dig.'

First we found the ferret on its line and then we pulled out nine rabbits. By dinner-time we had twenty-five, then after dinner we went up on Spring Hill, high on Bredon, and set snares in the rabbit runs. My job was to hammer in the pegs holding the wires with a little mallet.

At 6 o'clock that winter's night George and I climbed the hill with a carbide bicycle lamp, taking the snared rabbits from the wires. Forty of them.

At the back door Mr Bailey came out from his kitchen with his knife and paunched our catch, stringing them on sticks over the beams in the wash-house. I buried the paunches in the muck bury. Mr Bailey was never happier than when he was rabbiting.

Beetroot grows today where the rabbit warren was in Boss Close, and below irrigation pipes water the spring onions. I cycled to outlying fields at Old Manor Farm with my old boss. Now, Charles drives his Land Rover on made-up roads around the farm.

Time is money and the combine harvester lights up the corn fields at night as Charles or his one man, David, shears the stubble. Charles' eldest son is going to agricultural college and is interested in livestock. It would be good to see a dairy herd in the stalls at the farm.

Farming has become big business and the villages are no longer occupied by country people – yet in Tibblestone today that has not happened. Medium-sized farmers still work the land, despite the rules from Whitehall and Brussels. The set aside, the quotas, the throw-away society when implements are out of date in a few years and the village blacksmith no longer repairs the tools of the farm, may seem to be the rule of the day. In the Tibblestone Hundred there are still reminders of these days long ago, not necessarily better all round, for there must be change and there must be progress, but even so days when life on the land, its comings and goings, its ups and downs, were real and vital. It may not have had the modern machines of today, but it certainly had a quality all of its own.